Restoration Strab

Maynooth Studies in Local History

SERIES EDITOR Raymond Gillespie

This volume is one of five short books published in the Maynooth Studies in Local History series in 2007. Like their predecessors their aim is to explore aspects of the local experience of the Irish past. That local experience is not a simple chronicling of events that took place within a narrow set of administrative or geographically determined boundaries. Rather the local experience in the past encompasses all aspects of how local communities of people functioned from birth to death and from the pinnacle of the social order to its base. The study of the local past is as much about the recreation of mental worlds as about the reconstruction of physical ones. It tries to explore motives and meanings as well as the material context for people's beliefs. What held social groups together and what drove them apart are of equal interest and how consensus was achieved and differences managed can help to lay bare the lineaments of the local experience. The subject matter of these short books ranges widely. In the fraught world of the seventeenth century, in which religious division was endemic, communities in Cavan and Strabane managed to find enough common ground to make local worlds workable. Again in nineteenth-century County Dublin the desire for local improvement was sufficient to make the local government system triumph over political and religious division. Distress and division of another kind is evident in the emigration from nineteenth-century Ireland but the return of migrants with wealth and new experiences, an aspect of migration not much studied in the Irish context, helped to bind communities together again. Even in eighteenth-century Edenderry, on the Downshire estate, economic distress and political ferment in the 1790s strangely failed to produce military activity in the area in 1798. Understanding the common assumptions that held these communities together despite the tremendous pressures to which they were subjected is best done at the local level. Such communities remain the key to reconstructing how people, at many spatial and social levels, lived their lives in the past. Such research is at the forefront of Irish historical scholarship and these short books, together with the earlier titles in the series, represent some of the most innovative and exciting work being done in Irish history today. They provide models that others can use and adapt in their own studies of the local past. If these short books convey something of the enthusiasm and excitement that such studies can generate then they will have done their work well.

Maynooth Studies in Local History: Number 72

Restoration Strabane, 1660–1714

Economy and society in provincial Ireland

William J. Roulston

FOUR COURTS PRESS

Set in 10pt on 12pt Bembo by
Carrigboy Typesetting Services for
FOUR COURTS PRESS LTD
7 Malpas Street, Dublin 8, Ireland
e-mail: info@fourcourtspress.ie
http://www.fourcourtspress.ie
and in North America for
FOUR COURTS PRESS
c/o ISBS, 920 N.E. 58th Avenue, Suite 300, Portland, OR 97213.

ISBN 978–1–84682–060–1

Printed in Ireland
by ßetaprint, Dublin.

Contents

Acknowledgments

This book has had a long gestation stretching back to my undergraduate days when, under the tutelage of R.J. Hunter, then of the Department of History at the University of Ulster, I was introduced to the history of early modern Ulster. Later my studies were encouraged by W.H. Crawford, who directed me to the riches of the Public Record Office of Northern Ireland. Its former director, Brian Trainor, drew my attention to documents which have added considerably to my understanding of the period. Others to whom I am indebted include Michael Cox and John Dooher, both historians of some distinction of the Strabane area, and Raymond Gillespie and Toby Barnard who have done so much to cast light into the shadowy worlds of localities in the seventeenth and eighteenth centuries. I am especially grateful to Raymond for providing the opportunity to bring the results of my research to publication. I am grateful to the staffs at the following repositories for assistance in accessing and examining documents used in the course of my research: the Public Record Office of Northern Ireland, the National Archives of Ireland, the National Library of Ireland, the Registry of Deeds, and the Manuscripts Department at Trinity College, Dublin.

Introduction

L ife in provincial Ireland in the half century after the Restoration has not been a popular area of historical enquiry. Indeed, it may be said that the first half of the 17th century, particularly with regard to the northern province of Ulster, has been more carefully scrutinized by historians than the second. However, to quote Raymond Gillespie, 'much of the enduring legacy of seventeenth-century Ulster was forged, not in the first half of the century, but in the second'.[1] In emphasizing the importance of this period, he has drawn attention to a significant gap in Irish historiography. One field of study in which much work remains to be done is that of urban history. Again, it may be said that much more attention has been given to towns in the early 17th century than in the latter part of it.[2] In recent times the urban history of Ireland in general has become as increasingly popular area of study. In providing a range of cartographic materials, the fascicles produced by the Royal Irish Academy as part of the *Irish Historic Towns Atlas* series have created a basis for the further study of these settlements. Other areas of historical enquiry have also been pursued. Gillespie has considered the way in which a network of towns evolved in the course of the seventeenth century and the implications of this for the Irish economy.[3] Toby Barnard has done more than most to explore the urban society and culture in late 17th- and 18th-century Ireland.[4] However, few detailed case studies of Irish towns and their communities in the late 17th and early 18th centuries have so far been produced. The most thorough study of an urban community in this period is Jean Agnew's meticulous examination of the merchant families of Belfast.[5] Several volumes looking at individual towns in the 17th and 18th centuries have also been produced in the present series.[6]

The subject of this study is the town of Strabane from the Restoration to the death of Queen Anne, a period of just over fifty years. In the early 17th century the Strabane area was allocated to Scottish grantees under the plantation scheme. The subsequent settlement of hundreds of families from Scotland over the course of the next century has been the most significant demographic change in the area in the last four centuries and one that has had consequences which are still apparent today. The main aims of this investigation are to find out how the town functioned at social and economic levels and the physical setting within which it operated, how society was delineated and organized, and how the people of Strabane interacted with each other and the outside world. The first chapter will look

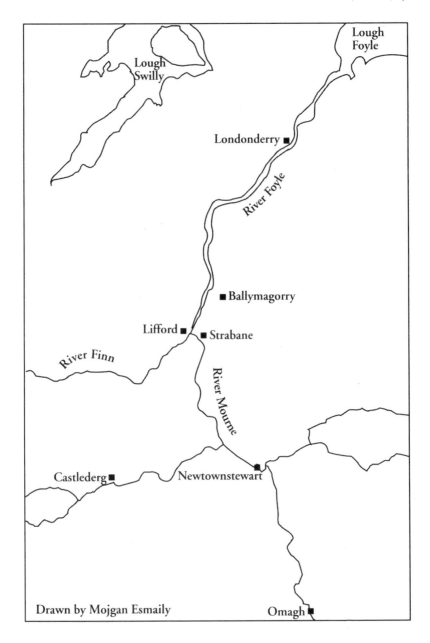

1 Strabane and north-west Ulster

at those individuals and institutions who exercised authority in the town in this period, namely the Hamilton landlords and the corporation. This will be followed by a chapter which will examine the population of Strabane as well as the topography of the town and economic developments during the period. The third chapter will attempt to sketch the contours of society in Strabane through a consideration of the different social groups which can be identified in the town. The final chapter will explore the different churches in the town and the religious controversy which arose from the tensions between the competing denominations.

The subjects covered in this study are to a large extent governed by the nature of the surviving source material. The Abercorn estate archive is less useful for this period than it is for later periods. Very little in the way of correspondence survives, but title and other deeds provide an insight into the way in which the estate evolved during this period, as well as information specific to some of the properties in the town of Strabane.[7] The extensive material in the Annesley collection in the Public Record Office of Northern Ireland relating to the Williamite land settlement is also useful in this regard.[8] The lives of the leading inhabitants of the town have been reconstructed using a variety of sources. In particular wills – both duplicate copies of the originals which perished in the destruction of the Public Record Office in Dublin in 1922 and abstracts made by genealogists, notably Tenison Groves, working in the Dublin PRO prior to that date – have proved extremely valuable. Research in the Registry of Deeds has also proved fruitful particularly with regard to exploring the topography and range of occupations in the town of Strabane in the early eighteenth century. The religious history of the town can be explored using a variety of sources. The correspondence of William King, bishop of Derry and afterwards archbishop of Dublin, provides not only an insight into the workings of the Church of Ireland, but also something of the relationship between Anglicanism and Presbyterianism.[9] No congregational records survive for the Presbyterian church in Strabane in this period, but the minutes of the Laggan presbytery are available for 1672–1700, while the minutes of the Synod of Ulster are available from 1691 onwards.

The history of Strabane in the early modern period has received attention in several previous publications. The early 17th century was covered by R.J. Hunter et al. in a publication that resulted from an extra mural course run through Magee University College in the 1970s.[10] Two decades later, one of Hunter's collaborators, Michael Cox, looked at developments in the seventeenth century for a volume providing a general history of Strabane produced by the local history society. The same work included two chapters by John Dooher on the 18th century as well as a chapter by the present writer which considers the origins of Presbyterianism in the area.[11] Eighteenth-century politics in the borough of Strabane have been expertly covered by Anthony Malcomson.[12] The present writer has already reconstructed the manorial network and changes in land ownership in the barony in the course of the 17th century.[13] As far as possible this study will try to avoid going over the same ground again.

1. Landlord and corporation

The question of authority and who exercised it was one of the key issues faced by society in early modern Ireland. Authority was represented and experienced in different ways by the various sections of the population. Most by reason of birth or religion were excluded altogether from the machinery of government in its various forms, whether central, local or parochial, while others were able to participate, but only in a limited way. In an urban settlement, particularly the new towns established as a result of the early 17th-century plantation scheme, the owner of the land on which the town stood could exercise considerable authority. His power to intervene and assist with the development of a town, however, was determined by a number of factors such as his security of title and economic position. In a borough town, authority could also be exercised by a corporation, the powers of which were determined by its charter. The ideal scenario was for the landlord and corporation to work in tandem to their mutual benefit, though this did not always happen. Interests could collide or the power of one could be rendered ineffective by the activities of the other. In any case, not every borough town had an active corporation. This chapter looks at the issues of authority and control in Strabane, focussing on the ownership of the town and of the role and composition of the corporation in this period. Other issues arising from the landlord's relationship to the town, concerning, for example, the layout and economic development of Strabane, will be examined in the next chapter.

The town of Strabane was in this period entirely within the bounds of the manor of the same name and because of this the ownership of the former was inextricably linked to that of the latter. The proprietorial history of Strabane in the 17th century is extremely complex, but unravelling it is essential to understanding how the town changed hands on several occasions even in the relatively short period covered by this study. At one level it seems straightforward enough. The owner of the manor and town in 1714 was a great-grandson of the original grantee in 1610. Both were named James Hamilton and both bore the title of earl of Abercorn. However, in the intervening period the estate was forfeited on three separate occasions with consequent repercussions for its ownership, while the Abercorn title was transferred between three separate lines of descent from the original holder.[1]

Under the terms of the scheme for the Plantation in Ulster, the barony of Strabane was allocated to Scottish grantees or undertakers, the chief of whom was James Hamilton, 1st earl of Abercorn, a personal favourite of James VI of Scotland. Abercorn was granted the great proportion of Dunnalong and the small proportion of Strabane. The latter included the demesne lands of Turlough Luineach O'Neill, a late 16th-century chieftain of the O'Neills. By 1613 the earl had acquired the proportion of Shean, bordering on the Strabane proportion, which had originally been granted to his brother-in-law, Sir Thomas Boyd. The 1st earl died in 1618 when his sons were still minors. According to an arrangement drawn up in 1620, the proportions of Strabane and Shean, now counted together as the manor of Strabane, were in time to devolve to Claud Hamilton, the second son of the 1st earl. Claud became Lord Strabane in 1633 on the resignation of the title by his elder brother James, 2nd earl of Abercorn, who had been provided with the Abercorn lands in Scotland as part of his inheritance. In the following year he was allowed to take formal possession of the manor of Strabane. Lord Strabane had married Lady Jane Gordon, daughter of the marquis of Huntly in 1632. He died in 1638 and was succeeded as 3rd Lord Strabane by his eldest son James.[2]

In one of the more bizarre episodes of the turbulent 1640s the widow of 2nd Lord Strabane married Sir Phelim O'Neill, one of the principal instigators of the 1641 rebellion. While still a youth, the third lord joined with his stepfather in open rebellion against the parliamentarian forces; he died a 'roman catholick and papist recusant' at Ballyfatton, near Strabane, on 16 June 1655. On account of his treason his lands were forfeited and in 1658 were in the possession of Edward Roberts, the Baptist auditor-general in Ireland.[3] His brother and successor, George, 4th Lord Strabane, was banished to Connacht early in 1657, though if he did go there he did not remain so for long, for in the so-called census of 1659 he was living in Swords parish, Co. Dublin.[4] Shortly before this Sir George Rawdon wrote of him, 'I fear there is little hope for Lord Strabane, who is under age and very poor.'[5] With the restoration of the monarchy in 1660 the 4th Lord Strabane was among those landowners restored to their respective estates at the king's command. Subsequent legislation in the form of the acts of settlement and explanation ratified the new land settlement. The 4th Lord Strabane died in 1668 and was succeeded by his eldest son Claud.[6]

Following the death of the childless 3rd earl of Abercorn in Italy around 1680, the earldom passed to Claud, Lord Strabane. The title was thus restored to the owner of the manor of Strabane. Other than enhancing his prestige and enabling the young Lord Strabane to sit in the Scottish parliament, it meant little because the Abercorn lands in Scotland had already been sold to cover debts owed there. The 4th earl was a leading supporter of James II. At the time of the 'Glorious Revolution' he accompanied the king to France and returned with him to Ireland. Arriving at Derry with his king in April

1689, the earl was reputedly 'horrified' to find that so many of his kinsmen and tenantry were among the city's defenders.[7] It was probably because of his connections with those inside the city's walls that he was sent into Derry to negotiate its surrender; however, his mission proved a failure. Soon afterwards, in a skirmish with some of the defenders outside the walls, he was wounded and had his horse shot under him. Following the Jacobite defeat at the battle of the Boyne, the earl was sent to France to appraise James of the situation in Ireland. However, near Brest his ship was attacked by a Dutch vessel and in the ensuing fight the earl was killed.[8] The 4th earl died unmarried and without heir and the earldom passed to his brother Charles. Although Claud was found guilty of high treason for his support for the Jacobite cause, and the Abercorn lands declared forfeit, the 5th earl was restored to the manor of Strabane on the express command of the king on 24 May 1692.[9]

The succession of the Abercorn estates was further complicated with the passing of the Act of Resumption in the English house of commons in 1700. This act annulled all of William III's land grants, including the grant of the manor of Strabane to the 5th earl of Abercorn. The act included provisions to protect the rights of those whose interest in the forfeited lands pre-dated 13 February 1689. Such individuals were obliged to register their claims with the Trustees of the Forfeited Estates in Ireland before 10 August 1700. To prove that he was the rightful representative of the male line of the family, the 5th earl was himself forced to submit a claim to the Trustees. He would probably have reacquired his estate had he not died without heir in June 1701.[10] The earldom then passed to his second cousin, Captain James Hamilton, now 6th earl of Abercorn. Soon afterwards he successfully petitioned to have the title of Viscount Strabane conferred on him as well.[11] On 1 September 1701 he was admitted as tenant of the manor of Strabane for one year ending the following May provided that he gave security to pay the Trustees or order within ten days after 1 May the rent for the demesne lands as they were currently set, as well as the reserved rents on the old leases and one year's value of the fee farm rents.[12] On 19 June 1703 the 6th earl purchased the town and manor of Strabane from the Trustees for £700.[13] The new owner of the manor of Strabane was the great-grandson of the 1st earl of Abercorn and grandson of Sir George Hamilton of Dunnalong. He had succeeded to his grandfather's estates in Strabane barony – comprising the manors of Cloghogall, Derrywoon and Dunnalong – on the latter's death in 1679 (his father having been died of injuries sustained during a naval engagement in 1673).[14] From this time on the ownership of the estate has remained remarkably stable with a smooth transition from one family member to the next right up to the present day.

Strabane was one of the new boroughs created in the early 17th century. Its charter of 1613 created a corporation consisting of a provost and twelve burgesses. The provost was to be elected annually, though there was nothing to stop one man from holding office for successive years, while the burgesses were life appointments. When a burgess died, the others were given the power to choose a replacement from the 'better or more worthy inhabitants of the borough'. The corporation was also permitted to appoint a recorder, chamberlain, constable, beadle, two sergeants-at-mace and an inspector of the grain market.[15] In the absence of a minute book or associated papers, it is impossible to provide any detail on the activities of the corporation of Strabane in this period. From the little evidence that has survived, however, it is clear that the corporation was an active body which contributed to the social and economic life of the town. Based on the few post-holders who are known, the office of provost was held by the leading inhabitants of the town. In 1669 the prominent merchant Patrick Hamilton was provost. Three generations of the McClenaghan family held the office of provost in this period: Andrew in 1675, his son David in the 1690s and David's son John in 1713.[16] The duties of the provost ranged from the ceremonial to the administrative. Among the tasks required was providing assistance in a variety of ways to any detachments of soldiers stationed in the town. For example, in 1664 the provost was ordered to 'take effectual order that necessary provision of fire and candle be made for the guards of such garrison as are placed in that town'.[17] The officers of the corporation included a town clerk (Hugh Brown in 1715) and town sergeant (James Cunningham in 1710).[18]

Information on who served on the corporation survives from two lists of burgesses. The earlier of these lists relates to the corporation appointed by James II on 8 August 1688 which comprised a provost, John O'Neill, and 23 burgesses, including, as was the case elsewhere, a number from the settler community: William Roe Hamilton, James Cunningham, James Hamilton, Robert Adams, Claud Hamilton, John Brown, Robert Gamble and James Magee.[19] Also included was Patrick Bellew of Old English background, and possibly Catholic. Given the disturbed state of the country at this time, it is unlikely that this corporation ever actually met. Of the Irish appointed to the corporation, few are known to have any connection with the town. Dominick McHugh was later listed among those Jacobites outlawed for treason where he is given the status of 'gent.' and styled of Strabane, but no other information is available on him.[20] Another of the Irish burgesses was Gordon O'Neill, son of Sir Phelim O'Neill and the widow of Claud Hamilton, second son of the 1st earl of Abercorn. Although through birth he belonged to the upper echelons of society, his economic position was at best akin to that of a member of the lesser gentry. He lived at Crew and possessed a lease of several townlands in the manor of Strabane; in 1691 the lease of these lands was valued at £320.[21] In 1681 he appears as the mortgagee of the freehold of Holyhill in Leckpatrick parish.[22] He conformed, ostensibly at any rate, for in the summer of 1680 Archbishop Oliver Plunkett wrote of him: 'Gordon O'Neill, the brother of Friar Phelim [O'Neill] and a nobleman, was a Catholic, but is now a Protestant, and his behaviour and way of life would lead one to expect a similar disaster [to that of his father?]'.[23] He fought with the Jacobite army at the battles of the Boyne and Aughrim, being severely wounded during the latter engagement and was subsequently outlawed for high treason.[24] By this time he was in exile in France where he fought with the Irish Brigade, dying there around 1704.[25] His daughter remained in Ireland, and in March 1701 the MP for Strabane, Oliver McCausland, appealed to Bishop King to intervene on her behalf.[26] This 'poor gentlewoman' had been living for some time with her aunt, Lady Lyndon, and afterwards in Co. Armagh with an Edward O'Hugh. He had promised to look after her, but was now attempting to force her to convert to Catholicism. What happened next is not known.

The Jacobite corporation was merely a brief interruption and soon after peace was restored in the north-west, the corporation was resurrected on its original lines with David McClenaghan as provost. When the town and manor of Strabane was vested with the trustees of the forfeited estates following the Act of Resumption of 1700, the members of the corporation were forced to take collective action to secure their interests. The claim of the provost and free burgesses of Strabane presented to the trustees of the forfeited estates in 1700 comprised the following names: David McClenaghan, provost, George McGhee, [–?] Patterson, Andrew Parke, David Cooke, James Berd, David Bradley, Thomas Browne, Thomas Maxwell, William Maxwell, John Gamble, John Browne, John Love, John Wilson and Robert Carson.[27] According to this list, there were 14 burgesses whereas the original charter stipulated that there were only to be 12. Most, but not all, of these men were merchants: McClenaghan possessed a substantial fee farm estate in the manor of Strabane, while McGhee was an apothecary.

During this period, the corporation was much more representative of the town's community that it was later to become with all of the burgesses resident in Strabane. By the 1730s the situation had changed considerably with burgesses being drawn from a wider range of people than the inhabitants of the town. In 1732 the provost, John Davis, lived at Mongavlin in Co. Donegal, and apart from being one of Abercorn's agents, had no real connection with the town. Several of the burgesses were the landowners or minor gentry in the north-west including William Forward of Castle Forward, Alexander Tomkins of Prehen and Hugh Edwards of Castlegore, but whose estates lay outside the barony of Strabane. The Hon. Charles Hamilton, son of the 6th earl of Abercorn and resident in England, was also a burgess as well as being one of the MPs for the town. This in itself was a departure from previous practice as before this there is no evidence that the MP for Strabane was also a member of the corporation. Of the 12 burgesses in 1732, eight were listed as being of Strabane, though for at least two of these men the connection was fairly tenuous. The number of merchants on the corporation had been reduced to two.[28] However, these changes do not seem to have been detrimental to the economy of the town which expanded rapidly in the 18th century. What they do reflect is a change from the days when the corporation was composed, in the main, of representatives from the merchant community serving the interests of that grouping. The process by which this change occurred is not clear. The 'Test Act' of 1704, which required all holders of civil and military offices under the crown to take communion in the Established Church, must have impacted upon the Strabane corporation in some way, but how is not known. It is possible that the Presbyterian burgesses in Strabane followed the actions of their co-religionists in Derry, and resigned en masse, though they could equally well have adopted the approach of the Presbyterian burgesses in Belfast and simply ignored the law for a few years.[29]

From the 1710s onwards the corporation was caught up in the struggle for power and influence between Oliver McCausland and his supporters and the 6th earl of Abercorn over the representation of the town at the parliament in Dublin. Very little is known of the selection or election of MPs for the borough of Strabane from this period and it is impossible to work out whether all those chosen to represent the borough were necessarily the nominees of the Hamiltons. One who certainly would have been was James Hamilton, probably the eldest son of Sir George Hamilton of Dunnalong, who was returned in 1666 to take the place of the recently deceased Sir Peter Harvey. If so, this is the first instance of the Hamiltons appointing a member of their own family as MP for Strabane. In 1692 the MPs returned for Strabane were Sir Matthew Bridges and Oliver McCausland. Bridges was styled 'of the city of Dublin' and, though described by Malcomson as a 'carpet-bagger', had some interests in the north-west, promising money towards the repair of Anglican chapels in Templemore parish.[30] McCausland was a local man and one of the most prominent figures in the north-west in this period.

He was the son of Alexander McCausland, one of the '49 officers, who had purchased the manor of Mountfield in Strabane barony from Sir Henry Titchbourne in 1658.[31] According to one source, these McCauslands were descended from a junior branch of the McAuslane family of Buchanan.[32] This suggestion is strengthened by a particularly strange letter McCausland received from a group of McCauslands in Kilbryd in Scotland.[33] Addressing him as 'Deir Cussing' and complaining that they were without a leader who could stand up for them when they wronged, they desired him to come over to Scotland to assume the headship of their clan. The hearth money roll includes several McCausland households in the parish of Cappagh, and it is possible that Alexander McCausland came from a family which had settled here. In 1675 Oliver inherited from his father the manors of Mountfield and Ardstraw, the latter a bishop's lease.[34] His first role in public life was his appointment in 1676 to the office of high sheriff of Co. Tyrone; he held this position again in 1691. The following year he became MP for Strabane. As far as his politics were concerned McCausland was a Whig. He did not, however, play an active part in the Irish house of commons, being nominated for only seven committees between 1692 and 1711. In 1695 he was hostile to Chancellor Porter who was accused by some MPs of favouring Catholics.[35]

One of the most interesting aspects of his career is the way in which he extended his landed base to something over 30,000 acres by the end of the first decade of the eighteenth century. Already the owner of the manor of Mountfield and the lessee of the manor of Ardstraw, in November 1692 he bought the reversion of several townlands in the barony of Tiranny in Co. Armagh from John Hamilton of Caledon.[36] In 1700 he completed the purchase of the Stranorlar estate in Co. Donegal.[37] Soon afterwards he formed an alliance with William Conolly to jointly purchase the manor of Castlefinn in that county.[38] He was keen to develop these lands and in 1711 acquired a patent for a Thursday market and four annual fairs to be held at Stranorlar.[39] In 1718 he was described as a 'man of interest, probity and prudence'.[40] Whereas his father had married a daughter of Edward Hall of New Grange, Co. Meath, Oliver chose a wife from a family based the northwest, marrying Jane, daughter of Revd James Hamilton, rector of Donagheady and archdeacon of Raphoe.

When exactly the relationship between McCausland and Abercorn began to deteriorate is not clear, though it was probably after and as a result of the earl's switch in political affiliations from the Whig to the Tory camp. Certainly at one point the two men were on cordial terms. In the autumn of 1704 Abercorn described McCausland as a 'special, good old friend', and was prepared to honour a promise made to him of a grant of land near Strabane.[41] After 20 years as an MP, McCausland had firmly established himself as the senior representative of the borough. In advance of the 1713 election it was predicted that the members for Strabane would be McCausland 'and whoever he brings in'. By this time Abercorn was beginning to make a concerted effort to have at least one of his nominees returned for Strabane. In March 1714 he wrote to the burgesses of Strabane at a time when Queen Anne's failing health had given rise to heightened expectations that a general election was in the offing. He asked the burgesses that they would return one nominee of his, promising that this individual would serve the interests of the town, and granting them liberty to choose whomsoever they wished as the second nominee, provided that person was not politically opposed to the earl. Privately Abercorn admitted that his offer to the burgesses was made on the basis that he was unlikely to be able to persuade them to leave out McCausland 'who lives among them'.[42] In the event his initial suspicions were proved correct and McCausland was re-elected. Abercorn did at least have the satisfaction of seeing his nominee, the Hon. Richard Stewart, younger brother of Lord Mountjoy, elected as the second MP for the borough. McCausland continued to serve as MP for Strabane until his death in 1723.

To what extent the leading inhabitants of the town participated in government at county level is impossible to retrieve due to the absence of grand jury records for Co. Tyrone from this period. An office occasionally held by the townsmen of Strabane was that of high sheriff of Co. Tyrone. Those who served in this capacity were Oliver McCausland (1676 and 1691), John Moderwell (1678), Patrick Hamilton (1679), Thomas Maxwell (1681) and John Gamble (1706). However, whatever prestige may have been attached to the post was frequently offset by the onerous nature of the duties it placed on the individual. The regularity with which the leading merchants of Strabane held the office of high sheriff in the late 1670s and early 1680s was a source of annoyance both for the individuals concerned and the wider community. The earl of Abercorn was persuaded to intervene and in late December 1681 he wrote to the lord lieutenant, the duke of Ormond, on behalf of Thomas Maxwell, who had been high sheriff that year and who was requested to continue as such for the incoming year.[43] Abercorn pointed out that it was 'a great hardship for one that lives by his calling to be forced to attend public employments so long, and it has gone fair to ruin the trade of this town, people being cautious to traffic where the sheriff resides if under any fears'. Abercorn's letter had the desired effect and Maxwell did not continue as high sheriff in 1682. The case illustrates the fact that while participation in public affairs was an indicator of status, the rewards were often negated by the costs.

2. Population, topography and economy

After Derry, Strabane was the most important town in north-west Ulster. Its location near the confluence of the rivers Mourne and Finn, serving a large hinterland in counties Tyrone and Donegal, and its proximity to the port of Derry all contributed to its importance. In the late medieval period Strabane was the site of an O'Neill castle, but was of relatively little importance in the Gaelic world. Following the implementation of the plantation scheme, it quickly grew into one of the main urban settlements in Ulster and by 1618–19 there were 80 houses in the town many of which were 'of lime and stone, very well and strongly built'.[1] The town benefited from the initial patronage of the 1st earl of Abercorn and subsequently that of his successors. In 1641 it was described by the mayor of Derry as 'a populous town and the best market in this country', albeit in a petition to have some of the burden of a large garrison transferred to the Strabane.[2] The town was captured by rebel forces in December 1641 and suffered as a result of the disturbances of the 1640s. By the mid 1650s, however, recovery was underway. According to the Civil Survey, the town of Strabane was 'rebuilded upon the ruins of the late devastation and repeopled with British inhabitants'.[3]

The reconstruction of the town in the 1660s was promoted by the town's landlords. Surviving deeds indicate that leases of tenements were granted to assist with the reconstruction. For example, when David Maghee was granted in fee farm several parcels of land in the town, among the 'divers good causes' mentioned was the 'replanting of the town of Strabane burnt in the late rebellion'.[4] What no doubt helped the recovery process was the continued presence in the town of several families who had first settled there in the early seventeenth century. In the mid 1680s, when Hugh Hamill wished to confirm as genuine a transaction from the 1630s, where the original deed was lost, he named several individuals as 'men alive in Strabane that can prove it'.[5] Appearing before an investigation into the ownership of a tenement in Strabane in 1676, Thomas Browne declared that his family had 'upheld it ever since the Plantation of Strabane town at which time about 60 years ago … James Brown senior [his grandfather?] came to Ireland with the Right Honourable James, late earl of Abercorn, or soon after'.[6]

The population of Ulster as a whole grew rapidly in the period after 1660, though, for a variety of reasons, there were regional variations in the rate of growth. Estimating the population of Strabane in this period has its difficulties as there is no reliable or comprehensive census data available. Unfortunately the so-called 'census of 1659' does not survive for Co. Tyrone. It is also impossible to estimate fully the impact of the upheavals of the 1640s on the demographics of the area. In 1660 the manor of Dunnalong, in the parish of Donagheady to the north of Strabane, was described as 'totally depopulated and devastated'.[7] However, the evidence of the poll tax book for Donagheady, dating from *c.*1661–2, would suggest that the manor was far from depopulated.[8] Comparable statistical data for the area as a whole is provided in the hearth money roll for 1666. The number of houses taxed in each parish in Strabane barony is shown in Table 1. Using the multiplier of 5.25 persons per household, this produces a total population of roughly 3,600. The hearth money rolls are, however, considered a fairly inaccurate tool for estimating total population. Trevor Carleton has compared the hearth money roll of 1666 with an earlier one of 1664, which survives for only four parishes in Strabane barony, and found over 50 per cent of the names recorded in 1664 are missing in 1666.[9] The next opportunity to examine the population of the area comes in a poll tax of 1696. The poll tax for Strabane barony was £339 12*s.* 11½*d.*[10] Working on the basis of a levy of 12*d.* per head, as laid down in the Poll Money Act, this gives a total adult population in the barony of around 6,800.[11] While this represents a rise in population from the 1660s, the increase was not as significant as that seen in other parts of Ulster, such as the Lagan Valley and north Armagh.[12]

Table 1. Households recorded in the hearth money roll of 1666

Parish	Households	British	Irish
Ardstraw	152	95	57
Badoney	117	20	97
Camus-juxta-Mourne	95	83	12
inc. Strabane	79	76	3
Cappagh	77	38	39
Donagheady	130	90	40
Leckpatrick	55	40	15
Urney	59	44	15
Total	**685**	**410**	**275**

To what can the increase in population be attributed? Essentially it comes down to two things: immigration and natural growth. Unfortunately, little can be said about either in Strabane. There was undoubtedly further settlement, particularly of Scots, in the 1660s and 1670s and again in the

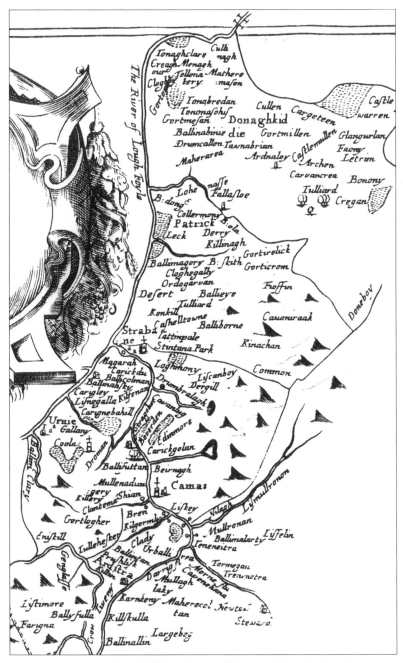

2 Extract from William Petty's *Hiberniae Delineatio* (1685)
showing Strabane area

1690s – waves of migration which can be traced elsewhere – but very little can be said about this either in pure statistical terms or in anecdotal evidence and family case histories.[13] The absence of church registers of any denomination for Strabane or the parish of Camus creates a difficulty in this regard which cannot be overcome.

In terms of the overall settlement pattern in north-west Tyrone in this period, Strabane stood at the centre of the main area of British settlement. Population was, of course, not evenly spread throughout the barony, while there were also clear areas of differentiation between districts where those of British origin and those of Irish background predominated. British settlement was heaviest in the low-lying area north and south of the town of Strabane and along the valleys of the Derg, Strule and Owenkillew rivers. Table 1 shows that the parishes of Ardstraw, Camus, Donagheady, Leckpatrick and Urney all had clear majorities of British households. Here was the best quality land. Irish settlement, by contrast, was concentrated on the higher, and consequently poorer quality, land. Much of the land in Badoney parish was mountainous and here more than 80 per cent of householders paying hearth tax were of Irish origin. British settlement in this parish was almost exclusively confined to a small number of townlands in the area around Gortin.

The town of Strabane was by far the largest settlement in the barony of Strabane. This is clearly demonstrated in the hearth money roll of 1666 where, apart from the village of Newtownstewart, there was not a single townland with more than seven householders paying hearth tax – the largest number of British householders in one townland was four.[14] Newtownstewart was essentially an estate village founded by Sir Robert Newcomen and Sir William Stewart in the early seventeenth century.[15] It was described in the mid 1650s as 'a market town in times of peace, but now not much frequented'.[16] In 1666 there were only eleven householders paying hearth tax in Newtownstewart; its total population would have been well under 100.[17] Some redevelopment took place in the late 17th century and the residence of Lord Mountjoy in the village undoubtedly contributed to this.[18] However, it was still only a 'small village' when Thomas Molyneux passed through it in 1708.[19] The only other nucleated settlement of any consequence in the Strabane area was at Ballymagorry, about three miles north of the town. It was another estate village, this time founded by Sir George Hamilton of Greenlaw, and, though it did not have a market, a patent to hold an annual fair here was granted in 1630.[20]

In 1666 there were 79 householders in Strabane paying hearth tax.[21] Using a multiplier of 5.25 persons per household and taking into consideration exemptions and evasions, Strabane probably had a total population of nearly 500 persons. It was by far the largest town in Co. Tyrone and one of the largest in Ulster. However, according to one classification, Strabane still only enjoyed 'small town' status in Ireland as a whole.[22] How quickly it grew in the fifty years after this is not known. There is little indication that it was devastated by events in the period 1689–91 to the extent that it had been in the 1640s. In the visitation carried out by Bishop William King in 1693 Strabane was described as a 'considerable town' – certainly it was the second largest town in Derry diocese.[23] In 1783 the population of the town was reckoned to be around 3,000.[24] Allowing for a significant increase in population in the middle decades of the 18th century when Strabane was the major centre for the linen industry in the north-west, it is possible that the number of inhabitants in the town was approaching the 1,000 mark in the mid 1710s. Yet its position as one of the principal market towns in the north of Ireland in the early 18th century did not earn favourable comment from contemporaries used to more mature urban developments. In 1719 the bishop of Derry, William Nicolson, a native of Cumberland in the north of England, remarked to the archbishop of Canterbury that Strabane was a 'small borough town', while in 1724 he described it as one of the 'little borough towns' of his diocese; in comparison with urban settlements in England Strabane was a relatively minor town.[25]

Of the houses recorded in 1666, one was taxed on three hearths, 12 houses paid tax on two hearths and the rest on only one hearth. In terms of accommodation Strabane ranked fairly poorly in comparison with other towns in Ulster. In many of the other small towns in Ulster there were higher numbers of houses with at least three hearths. For example, in Ballymena there were three houses with three or more hearths, while in Glenarm there were eight.[26] In Strabane's rural hinterland the housing was similarly modest. In fact, in the whole of Strabane barony there were only three houses outside of the town of Strabane with two hearths and none with more than two.

There are no detailed maps of Strabane surviving any earlier than the first edition Ordnance Survey of the 1830s, nor is there a detailed estate survey surviving from this period. This is a major obstacle to attempting to plot the layout of the town in the early 18th century. Although listed among the walled towns in Ireland in 1657, Strabane had no defensive perimeter – possibly some temporary barricades had been erected during the 1640s – and was an essentially open town.[27] A sketch map of 1659 shows the town as essentially one long street with a castle about two-thirds of the way along it, while there also appears to be a representation of a market cross. This street, which can be equated with present-day Main Street, ran roughly north-south, and the castle was on a site opposite the junction of Castle Street with Castle Place.[28] The castle was the most important building in Strabane in this period. Originally built by the 1st earl of Abercorn and considerably extended by the widow of Lord Strabane in the 1630s, it had been occupied by both sides in the fighting of the 1640s. It evidently suffered some damage as it was not in repair at the time of the Civil Survey of 1654–6. It does not appear in the hearth money roll of 1666, but must have been repaired in the latter part of the 17th century when it was the home of the 4th and 5th earls of Abercorn, the latter dying in it in 1701.[29] After that it seems to have been abandoned and there is no evidence that the 6th earl of Abercorn ever lived there.

The public buildings in the town were represented by the two churches – Church of Ireland and Presbyterian – and the market house. The Church of Ireland church is represented on the 1659 map; this church was in the graveyard at the junction of Patrick Street and Church Street. It had been started by the 1st earl of Abercorn prior to his death in 1618. The graveyard attached to it was the main place of burial for the inhabitants of the town. Several of them specified interment in the 'Church yard of Strabane' in their wills; James Hamilton, who died c.1703, requested to be buried there 'in decent manner'.[30] The first Presbyterian meeting house is likely to have been built in the town in the 1670s. The deed of 1712 conveying the site for a new church refers to the previous meeting house as having been on 'the west side of the Bowling Green'. The site – with the new meeting house already standing on it – was towards the southern end of the town on 'the High Street leading from the said town to the mill of Strabane'.[31] The market-house was also on the south side of Strabane. It had probably been newly constructed in the years after the Restoration under the patronage of the Hamilton landlords of the town. It was certainly in existence in 1679 when it is referred to in a deed.[32] It provided an important focus for economic activity of the town and in front of it was the market place. There were few buildings or premises in the town associated with small scale industrial activities. A 'brewhouse' belonging to John Anderson is mentioned in a deed of 1697, while a tan house and tan pits and a malt house are mentioned in early 18th-century deeds.[33] There were also a number of inns which provided lodgings for travellers.[34] Although a sessions house had been built by 1622, Strabane was never an assize town; the sessions house was probably destroyed in 1641 and not rebuilt.

For any town to be an effective marketing centre it required good communication links with the outside world. Little in the way of information on the roads in the north-west has survived from this period. The topography of the surrounding district meant that the main approaches to Strabane were from the north and south. There were two ways of approaching the town from the south, along either the western or eastern sides of the river Mourne. If the former route was chosen the last part of the journey to the town would have been by ferry and then, from the mid 1690s, by a bridge. If the latter route was taken the Mourne would have been crossed further upstream, and the journey would have passed the ruins of the former medieval parish church at Camus and then Strabane mill. The road leading north from Strabane passed through the village of Ballymagorry and connected the manors of Cloghogall and Dunnalong to the town. It also provided a route to the Waterside of Derry from where people and goods could be ferried across the Foyle to the walled city. To what extent the river Foyle was used a communication link between Strabane and Derry in this period is unclear. Some light boats may have been able to sail as far as Strabane at certain times of the year, but larger vessels certainly would not have been able to do so. The town was connected to its Donegal hinterland on the other side of the river Foyle via Lifford. Again, the crossing would have been initially by ferry and subsequently by a bridge.

It has already been noted that the proprietor of the manor of Strabane was the owner in fee simple of the land on which the town of Strabane stood. In 1622 the townsmen had petitioned for some land for free burgage and common, but no such allocation seems to have been made.[35] The pattern and layout of the tenements in Strabane had been largely determined by the leasing policy of the town's landlords in the pre-1641 period. Lessees of property in Strabane received a grant in fee farm of a tenement in the town and a small parcel of land just beyond the town limits in what became known as the 'town parks'. The Civil Survey noted that the lands on which the town stood were 'let in tenements and acres to the inhabitants of the corporation, to most of them in fee farm'.[36] Fee farms were holdings leased in perpetuity at a fixed annual rent. This generally combined a cash sum with a requirement to provide specified livestock at certain times of the year. The granting of a proportion of their estates in fee farm was a basic requirement of the English and Scottish grantees who received lands as part of the Plantation scheme.[37] In Scotland, 'feuing' as a tenure had existed on church lands from the twelfth century and became much more widespread from the fifteenth century onwards. In England, the holding of land in freehold had been an important and prized tenure in the manorial system.[38] The inclusion of fee farm grants among the required tenures in the Ulster Plantation scheme has been viewed as a means of introducing substantial tenants to an estate who would form the backbone of rural society. The disadvantage was that having granted a fee farm the landowner lost all future economic potential in those lands since the rent remained the same no matter how much the lands in question increased in value.

After 1660 the town's landlords continued to grant tenements and town parks in fee farm, including over a dozen leases issued on 30 April 1676.[39] In 1681 the 4th earl of Abercorn wrote that his tenants in the town 'have no land or estates but their "marchendising" substance and inconsiderable town freeholds'.[40] In 1700 over 50 fee farm interests relating to the town of Strabane were entered with the trustees of the forfeited estates, from lessees anxious that their interests should be protected following the forfeiture of the manor of Strabane by the 5th earl of Abercorn.[41] It would seem that granting tenements in fee farm was the preferred option for the town's landlords in the 17th century and was a practice continued by the 6th earl of Abercorn in the years immediately after his purchase of the manor of Strabane in 1703.[42] Much has been made of the building lease as a device used by landlords to encourage urban development in this period. Such a lease would contain a covenant requiring the tenant to construct a house of certain dimensions, structure and roof covering. However, building leases do not seem to have been used in Strabane. Certainly, those fee farm grants which survive do not contain building covenants. Even in the widespread use of perpetuity leases, Strabane differed from other towns in Ulster. In Lurgan, for example, more than half of the leases granted in 1667 were for less than ten years and it was only gradually that these short leases were replaced with longer ones.[43] Elsewhere in Ulster, landlords were attempting to develop towns by offering attractive leases to potential tradesmen.[44] For example, at Glenarm in Co. Antrim, Alexander MacDonnell issued over 20 leases to a range of individuals between 1672 and 1679. However, these leases were for a determinate number of years and included building covenants.[45] Further research on Ulster towns in general in this period would be needed to judge whether the leasing policy of the Hamiltons in Strabane was typical or atypical of urban development in the province as a whole.

Fee farm tenancies were secure and prized holdings. Undoubtedly the granting of much of Strabane in fee farm tenements in the pre-1641 period contributed to the continuity of the town between the first and second halves of the 17th century. Although many of the deeds were lost or destroyed as a result of the disruption caused by the 1641 rebellion – the castle in Strabane seems to have been used as a repository for such documents – most of the tenancies continued to be recognized as such because there were those who could attest to their existence.[46] There were, however, a number of disputes over property and its ownership. In one particular case from 1675–6 it was pointed out that because of the vicissitudes of the Hamilton family, new deeds to replace those which had been lost had never been issued.[47] It is possible that the large number of leases issued in April 1676 was to replace deeds lost in 1641, though this would be difficult to prove. There was an active market in the sale and purchase of fee farm tenements in Strabane, providing, in some instances, links with the outside world. For example, surviving from September 1698 is a deed concerning a tenement in Strabane involving Margaret Mackan of Ballygilgan, County Sligo, widowed daughter of the late Robert Lawley the younger, formerly of Jamestown, Co. Leitrim, a butcher, and William Lawley of the town of Sligo, a baker, son and heir of the late William Lawley of Strabane, a butcher.[48] There is some evidence that the Hamiltons tried to regulate the sale of fee farms. For example, when Hugh Hamill purchased a fee farm that had been originally been granted to James Patton it was to the annoyance of the 4th earl of Abercorn; the dispute was resolved when Hamill agreed to pay the earl £3, being a year's rent of the property.[49] Landlords, particularly those who were frequently absent from their estates needed effective and trustworthy agents. One who fulfilled this role for around fifty years was David McGhee, agent on the Hamilton-owned manors of Strabane and Cloghogall.[50] His background is unclear, but he was possibly the son of John 'Macghee' who died in 1618 and is buried in the old graveyard at Leckpatrick, where his tombstone can still be seen. He was probably appointed agent in the mid to late 1620s following the death of an earlier agent, William Lynne, in 1625. By 1628 he had been appointed the seneschal of the manor of Strabane.[51] During the 1650s he attempted to continue the management of the Strabane estates of the Hamiltons despite the uncertainty of the period.[52] McGhee himself possessed the freehold of Balliburny, or Holy Hill, in the manor of Cloghogall to the north of Strabane. The Civil Survey describes him as a 'Scottish Papist' though this was obviously no bar to representing the interests of an absentee landlord in Strabane barony.[53] Indeed, it may have been this very fact that first brought him into the service of the family of Sir George Hamilton of Greenlaw, himself a prominent Catholic in the barony. Macghee died 'on or about' 9 October 1678 and left a nuncuputative will which provides a good deal of additional information on his family and property.[54] To his wife Catherine he left all the rents arising out of the lands of Loghmony and Drumnaboy as well as the houses and lands in the town of Strabane for the rest of her natural life. Following her death, these were then to pass to his eldest son George. In the 1690s the 5th earl of Abercorn had several agents including John Henderson, who in December 1701 was instructed by the trustees of the forfeited estates to state the value of the rents he had collected in the manor on behalf of the earl.[55]

The fact that most of Strabane was held by perpetual tenancies had a knock-on effect on the rental value of these tenements for the town's landlords. In a rent roll of the manor of Strabane from *c.*1702 the income from the tenements in the town was put at £137 6s. 9d.[56] This represents a modest 18 per cent of the total income derived from the manor of Strabane, a far lower proportion than some urban rentals in other parts of Ulster. For example, the urban rents from Sir Arthur Brownlow's estate in north Armagh contributed to more than half of his total income in 1675.[57] As rents on farmland increased in the course of the 18th century, the proportion of the freehold town rents to the overall rents of the manor of Strabane fell even more sharply so that by 1800 it was less than 5 per cent.[58]

The town parks themselves were an important asset to those who held them. Some included small orchards which not only provided a useful food supply, but were also viewed as a feature which enhanced the environment.[59] The individual parks were divided by a network of lanes and occasionally by hedges or even walls. One was partly enclosed by a 'hedge of sallies and gooseberry bushes'.[60] During this time, the town was more or less confined to the eastern side of the Mourne. There had been some attempts to develop the western side of the river with fee farm grants issued for several small properties in Ballycolman. At what dates these leases were made is not known, but by the mid 1690s this townland contained three holdings of two acres each possessed by John Love, William Maxwell and Hugh Brown, as well as a house, garden and orchard in the possession of Patrick Fleming, all of them merchants in Strabane.[61]

One of the most significant additions to the infrastructure of the town, and one which at least opened up the possibility of further development on the western side of the Mourne, was the construction of a bridge over the river in 1696–7. Bishop King of Derry took a keen interest in the project and wrote a lengthy and detailed letter to the 5th earl of Abercorn on the deliberations relating to the site of the bridge which not only provides an insight into the socio-economic conditions prevailing in the town, but also allows for a glimpse at the topography of Strabane at this time. In late October 1696 King visited Strabane where he met with Abercorn's agent, Mr Hamilton, the provost of the town and a large number of the inhabitants. There was a difference of opinion between Hamilton and the majority of the townspeople over the site of the bridge. Hamilton wanted it opposite to the castle believing that it was important that Abercorn as proprietor of the town should be able to see the bridge from his house. He was also of the opinion that the bridge should be built below some waste tenements in order to encourage their reuse. If this area was revitalized it could yield Abercorn £25 per annum which would help to offset the loss of earnings from the leasing of the ferry. King agreed with him on this, but disagreed with his first argument believing that if the bridge were built here it 'would make the passage to your Lordship's house the great thoroughfare of the town'.

King then asked the provost and townspeople why they objected to Hamilton's proposed site. They replied that it was unlikely that the tenements in question were going to be rebuilt because their owners were poor and had in fact been out of repair from before the troubles of 1688–91. Because they had been mortgaged and yet produced no income, it was going to be difficult to clear the debts on them. Another objection from the townspeople was that building the bridge where Hamilton wanted would increase the risk of flooding in the town. They produced a certificate from the workmen engaged to built the bridge which indicated that building the bridge on Hamilton's site could potentially mean that during exceptional rainfall some houses would be flooded to a depth of seven feet. Not only would this further hinder the repair of the waste tenements; it would also render uninhabitable several houses which were already occupied.

Furthermore, the articles of agreement drawn up with the workmen allowed them to choose one of three sites, yet the one on which Hamilton wanted to build the bridge was not one of these. This, together with the additional cost of building the bridge in deeper water, further militated against Hamilton's choice of site. Having weighed up all the arguments, King himself was inclined to agree with the townspeople's choice of site – which incidentally was also favoured by Abercorn – but deferred the final decision to the earl. In any case, the foundations could be not be laid before the end of that year. The outcome in relation to the choice of site is not known, but the construction of the bridge proceeded and was completed by the following summer at a cost of £500.[62]

Not surprisingly, given the settlement history in the barony as a whole, the population of Strabane was dominated by Scots. There was, however, at least one family of Old English in Strabane in the 17th century: the Bellews. A deed probably dating from the mid 1660s mentions 'Richard Bellew deceased'.[63] The 1666 hearth money roll includes a Widow Bedloe, very possibly a corruption of Bellew, and if so likely to have been the wife of Richard. A Patrick Bellew, possibly their son, was appointed a member of the corporation of Strabane during the reign of James II. He owned a house in Church Street which he subsequently sold to Robert Baird.[64] What should have brought an Old English family to Strabane is unclear, though it was quite possibly through connections established by the Hamilton land-lords of the town. The Gaelic Irish population in the town of Strabane in this period was all but invisible. A few scattered references occur, but nothing to show that the Irish occupied anything other than a fairly low position in the general scheme of things. This represents a change from the early 17th century where in certain areas individual Irishmen could exercise consider-able influence. There is no example of a Patrick groom O'Devin, the lessee of the entire Manor Eliston estate for a period in the 1610s, after 1660.[65]

The hearth money roll of 1666 includes only one man with an obviously Gaelic Irish name, John McGuire, though James McCaskey may well have been another. A deed of 1681 refers to 'eight houses wherein Thomas O'Managhan and others dwells [*sic*] above [where] ye meeting house stands'.[66] A house occupied by Knogher McMurierty is mentioned in a deed of 1683.[67] He was clearly of some importance for he was included among the Irish Jacobites outlawed for high treason, where he is styled 'yeoman'.[68] Also outlawed for high treason from Strabane were Patrick Bellew, gent., James Farrell, yeoman and Dominick McHugh, gent. Occasionally Irishmen turn up as witnesses to deeds including Phelim Mullans in 1662 and Da. Divine in 1705.[69]

Likewise, though for different reasons, the English population was virtually negligible. Only a few men with English names turn up in Strabane in this period, and none occupied a particularly prominent position. Houses occupied by Edward Chadwick and John Elkin are mentioned in the will of Patrick Hamilton senior in 1659. There was only one significant English family in the Strabane area during this period: the Babingtons of Urney, lessees of the bishop's lands in the parish of Urney, a substantial holding of several thousand acres. The Babingtons had been tenants of the Urney bishop lands from the early 17th century and were probably of the same family as Brutus Babington, briefly bishop of Derry, 1610–11. A story that Richard Babington, the first of the family in Urney, was the bishop's son remains unproven. In the 1650s the lessee in Urney was Mathew Babington, Richard's executor and probably his son. In a rental of the bishopric of Derry of *c*.1696 the Babingtons were described as 'honest good people' who had 'improved the farm very well'.[70] They seem to have had very little interaction with the inhabitants of Strabane and looked beyond this part of Co. Tyrone for marriage partners and land acquisitions.

The latter part of the 17th century was a period of major restructuring in the Irish economy as it became increasingly specialized. In particular there was a move away from the export of raw materials in favour of processed goods. The Cattle Acts of the 1660s which banned the live export of cattle from Ireland to England were instrumental in accelerating this development, though there were indications of a shift in the economy even before this.[71] Trades and industries which had previously been of secondary importance now rose in importance. These included the butter trade and, even more importantly as far as the long term prosperity of Ulster was concerned, the linen industry. The latter was to be of particularly significance to Strabane. Geographical factors meant that the town in the early modern period was part of an economic region centred on the Foyle Valley with its focus on the city and port of Derry and with strong links to eastern Co. Donegal.[72] To the east of Strabane the Sperrins mountain range has acted as a physical barrier to the full economic and social integration of Strabane with the rest of Tyrone and in particular the east of the county and the towns of Cookstown and Dungannon.

A small merchant community had been established at Strabane in the 1610–41 period and in 1613 the town's charter allowed for a weekly market and two annual fairs.[73] In the early 18th century, though probably beyond the period covered by this study, the increase the town's trade necessitated the holding of a second weekly market.[74] The weekly market was vital as the outlet for the distribution of surplus agricultural produce from the town's hinterland and the means by which necessities, which could not be produced locally, could be acquired by the local community. Strabane was ideally placed to be the focus of economic activity over a wide area. In Co. Tyrone the nearest market to Strabane was at Newtownstewart around eight miles away. There was a market at Lifford in Co. Donegal barely two miles from Strabane. Lifford was, however, a much smaller settlement than

Strabane – only 68 poll tax payers in 1659[75] – and the two towns were separated by the river Foyle. Derry was a further fifteen miles beyond this. Two fairs a year were also held in Strabane, providing further opportunities for trade and commerce. While the troubles of the 1640s had caused severe disruption to the Irish economy, those of 1689–91 did not have quite the same impact. The period of actual warfare was shorter and more localized in its impact. As a result of the siege of Derry and associated encounters between Williamite and Jacobite, the Foyle valley was probably one of the more affected areas. If Bishop King's estimates are to be believed, there were only 300 out of 250,000 cattle in the diocese of Derry once peace had been restored. However, large numbers of livestock were imported from Scotland in the 1690s, preventing famine from breaking out.[76]

The merchant community in Strabane in this period was probably quite small, perhaps no more than a dozen to twenty men who can truly be recognized as individuals who engaged in trade and commerce. Of these, only a handful had interests which extended beyond the north-west. Frustratingly little has survived about their businesses. It is perhaps not insignificant that Jean Agnew in her meticulous study of the Belfast merchant community in the 17th century has absolutely nothing to say about trading links with Strabane.[77] Only four merchants' trade tokens have been identified for Strabane from the period 1654–79.[78] These were issued by John Brown, James Coninghame, John M[–?] (possibly Moderwell) and Claud [?]t (possibly Scott). If these suppositions are correct, all four men appear in the 1666 hearth money roll for Strabane. The number of trade tokens issued for a town has been used an indicator of the relative size of the merchant community. In Ulster the largest number of surviving tokens is for Belfast with 26 issuers followed by Derry with 18. Strabane belongs to a group which includes Ballymoney, Ballymena, Enniskillen and Newry, each of which had between four and six token issuers.[79] Judged on the number of deeds registered at the Registry of Deeds relating to Strabane, it is clear that there was considerable economic activity in the town in the early 18th century. In the period 1708–38 there were around four times as many deeds registered for Strabane as for Dungannon, while only a handful of deeds were registered for the other corporate towns in Co. Tyrone, Augher and Clogher.

Most overseas trade was almost certainly done through the port of Derry, though there is scant evidence to document this. It is likely, however, that the relationship between Strabane and Derry was something akin to that between Lisburn and Belfast, with one feeding off the other's trade.[80] Having to trade through Derry brought its own difficulties at different times due to the duties charged on the import of salt and export of butter through that port. Early in 1705 the Strabane merchants decided to take action against what they saw as an unfair burden on their business activities and

complained to the Derry corporation. The corporation responded by examining its own charter and coming to the conclusion that it had to continue
with these duties because it had to maintain the walls and gates of the city
out of its customs. Not satisfied with this answer, John Gamble, the provost
of Strabane, wrote to the mayor of Derry in early May 'in relation to the town's
custom taken from foreigners [i.e. anyone outside of Derry]'.[81] However, as
the corporation was still unwilling to act, Gamble, on behalf of the Strabane
merchant community, petitioned the Irish parliament arguing that

> Being obliged to enter their goods at the custom-house of Derry,
> they have by the by-laws of that corporation an extraordinary duty
> imposed on their merchandise, to wit, a fourth part in proportion to
> the duty payable to her Majesty by Act of Parliament on all salt
> imported, and the same on all butter exported, which is double what
> any other corporation takes; and the said increase of duty the
> petitioner conceives is illegal and tends to the discouragement of the
> small remaining trade of the said corporation.[82]

A parliamentary committee was appointed to look into the matter on 2 June
1705 and letters were issued summoning the mayor and chamberlain of Derry
to attend a meeting on 13 June. However, as there were reports that parliament
was about to be adjourned, the Derry corporation decided against sending the
two men, and the matter seems to have fallen into abeyance.[83] The fact that it
was not pursued may have been due, in part at any rate, to the fact that
Strabane's economic interests were going in a different direction.

For most of the 17th century the town's trade was predominantly in
agricultural produce. There were, therefore, close ties between Strabane and
its rural hinterland as crops harvested and livestock raised were marketed in
the town. Little is known of agricultural practices in the surrounding area,
though there are references to the grazing of cattle, while there were
sufficient numbers of sheep in the area to justify the presence of several
woollen or tuck mills.[84] The Civil Survey made the following comment on
the agricultural productivity of the land in Strabane barony: 'For the most
part mountainous and woody, chiefly east and southward only fit for pasture;
westward and on the rivers where it is arable the soil is but barren and only
fit for oats and summer barley.'[85] The acreage of cereal crops increased
substantially in the latter part of the 17th century so that by 1700 there were
mills at Seein, Tullywhisker, Strabane and Douglas in the manor of Strabane
alone – double the number in 1660 – which had a combined value of £57
10s.[86] Tenants were bound by their leases to grind their corn at the named
mill ensuring an income for the miller.

However, what made Strabane one of the leading trading centres in
Ulster in the 18th century was the rise of the linen industry. In the late

1730s it was described by one visitor as a 'large trading town' and the principal linen market in the north-west.[87] The origins of the linen industry in the area remain largely unknown. Some linen yarn was produced in the area in the early 17th century and was among the goods exported to Chester by two Strabane merchants in 1632.[88] However, the extent of this trade is not clear, and as much remains hidden about the initial development of the manufacture of and trade in linen in the area, it is not possible to explore the origins of this trade in Strabane in the way that Crawford was able to do in north Armagh.[89] Of some significance was the hosting of a textile exhibition in 'a large apartment made in the side of the town hall' in Strabane in 1700, a report of which was sent to James Hamilton, who the following year was to become 6th earl of Abercorn, by his agent. [90] One of the key aims of the exhibition was to encourage good practice in the manufacture of linen with, among other demonstrations, a display of girls spinning yarn like 'well-trained soldiers'. Those in attendance comprised the leading gentry and merchants in the district, as well as several individuals from further a field, including the bishop of Clogher and William Cairnes, a merchant and probably the Limerick-based son-in-law of William Maxwell.[91]

Abercorn's agent took a prominent role in the proceedings and was particularly concerned to avoid collusion between the judges and participants. This concern moved him 'to appoint (as the seven judges) the foremost persons ... merchants of good credit and discretion and known integrity'. While some merchants sat as judges, others took part in the competition. Those who won prizes included Hugh Hamilton of Drumgauty (£7 for a 'hollowa' web), Alexander Warnock of Rash (£4 for a 'mushlan') and Captain Robert Beard, styled 'of St Johnston' in Co. Donegal, but with property in Strabane (£5 for a 'tickin' web).[92] Spinning wheels were made available and carefully disposed of by the burgesses of Strabane principally to local women, some of them widows, though one recipient was an orphan, Thomas Brown. Although not explicitly stated, the disposal of wheels in this way may have been designed to provide a livelihood for those on the fringes of poverty.[93] The impression one gets from this exhibition is that of an industry which had already begun to establish itself in the district and in which there was considerable variety and a willingness to experiment with different manufacturing techniques and types of cloth.

The 6th earl of Abercorn himself actively promoted the linen industry in the Strabane area and, based on experiences elsewhere in Ulster, his involvement is likely to have been crucial to its local development. In 1708 Thomas Molyneux described Strabane as a 'somewhat better town' than its near neighbour Lifford and noted that here Lord Abercorn had encouraged the manufacture of linen.[94] If the evidence points to the earl as an encourager of the linen industry in Strabane, information on how exactly he did this is not forthcoming. It is, therefore, impossible to compare Abercorn's

contribution with that of, for example, Arthur Brownlow at Lurgan.[95] By
1711 Abercorn was a trustee of the Linen Board, as was Lord Mountjoy, the
owner of the neighbouring estate.[96] Years later in 1733 the 6th earl, by then
an old man, reflected on the fact that he had 'soon after that happy
revolution at my own great expense promoted the linen industry in that
neighbourhood and which has so far succeeded that at Strabane is now the
greatest staple of linen yarn in the Kingdom'. In other ways the 6th earl
tried to create a stable environment for economic growth. Following the
uncertainty created by the Williamite land settlement, he had respected the
property rights of those who had failed to register claims for tenements in
the town with the Trustees of the Forfeited Estates so long as they 'had a
mind to live therein'.[97]

Others were also showing some initiative. One who stood out for his
endeavours was John Henderson, invariably referred to as 'Captain' or 'Esq.'[98]
A deed of 1708 refers to his 'blechery' in the manor of Cloghogall,
presumably referring to an early bleaching operation. He was also a recipient
of grants totalling £180 from the Trustees for the Management of the Linen
Manufacture in Ireland between 1706 and 1708, suggesting that his business
was fairly extensive.[99] Henderson was in possession of several properties in
Strabane barony, including a fee farm of 'Flushtown and Foretown' in the
manor of Strabane, as well as lands in Co. Donegal; he had also served for
a time as the agent to the 5th earl of Abercorn.[1] In addition he had
connections with the Cairnes family in Co. Monaghan, themselves involved
in the early development of the linen industry in that county.[2] It may be
reasonably assumed that it was his landholdings, together with the above
grants, that provided the necessary capital that he needed to fund the initial
costs of his enterprises. At the same time it may not have succeeded for there
is no further mention of the bleach green in Cloghogall after this.
Henderson's activity in this area seems to have been unique among the local
gentry. Others may have been interested, but the steps they took, if any, to
promote the linen industry on their estates are not known. How and to
what extent the merchants in Strabane participated in the linen trade during
this period is also unclear, but the evidence from the exhibition discussed
above indicates that some were both interested and involved in the industry.

3. Urban society

Later Stuart society in Ireland was a complex series of layers, made all the more difficult to interpret by the frequent overlapping between them. Though regional studies of the structures of society are a well established part of English historiography, the same cannot be said for Ireland. Toby Barnard has done much to outline the contours of Protestant society in Ireland in the late 17th and 18th centuries and the material world within which it operated and some excellent regional studies have recently appeared.[1] Yet much remains to be more fully explored and understood, particularly with regard to the province of Ulster with its distinctly Presbyterian tinge.

Society in Strabane in this period ranged from the aristocracy to the beggars with the esquires, gentlemen, clerics, merchants, tradesmen and labourers in between. Distinguishing between the different groups is not as straightforward as it might appear. Esquire, for example, was the title generally given to a non-aristocratic landowner. However, at different times others, not owners of estates, were denoted esquire. The holding of public office of some description often resulted in the conferral of this title on the office-bearer, though only for so long as the position was held. For example, when John Moderwell and Patrick Hamilton were appointed commissioners of the poll tax ordinance of 1660 they were called 'esquires' even though both men were merchants in the town of Strabane. On the other hand, to emphasize the inconsistency with which such rules were applied, Alexander McCausland, the recent purchaser of an estate in the barony, was denoted a mere gentleman – itself a title that defies simple definition – in the same list.[2] In other cases it was possibly to ensure that the person so denoted would have greater respect afforded him. In 1705 when John Gamble petitioned the Irish parliament on behalf of the merchants in Strabane, he was given the title of esquire, though he himself was also a merchant, albeit a fairly wealthy one. What follows is a discussion of the different groups of which society in Strabane was composed in the latter part of the 17th century and early years of the 18th, starting, as is the convention, with those at the top.

The very top of the social order in Strabane is easy enough to identify. There was only one aristocratic family in Strabane in this period: the Hamiltons, the head of which held the title Lord Strabane and afterwards earl of Abercorn. Other than the traditional landlord-tenant relationships, this family had few connections with the other inhabitants of the town, or even the surrounding area for that matter. They avoided marriage with local families, preferring to establish marital connections with families from Dublin or England. The 4th and 5th Lords Strabane also differed from most of the townsfolk in that they were Catholics. George, 4th Lord Strabane, married a daughter of Christopher Fagan of Feltrim in Swords parish, Co. Dublin, a member of a wealthy Catholic gentry family which was already intermarried with aristocracy. In the so-called census of 1659 he and Fagan appear in Feltrim (Festryne).[3] His son, Claud, the 5th Lord Strabane and 4th earl of Abercorn, also looked to Dublin for a wife, though whether he ever secured a bride is doubtful; certainly he died without issue.[4] Charles, 5th earl of Abercorn, was a Protestant, though whether he had been brought up as such or had converted for purely opportunistic reasons to secure the return of the family estate in 1692 is unclear. The 6th earl was also a Protestant. The 5th and 6th earls looked to Britain and Dublin for wives. Charles married his cousin Catherine, the eldest daughter of James, 2nd earl of Abercorn. She had previously been married to William Lenthall. The 6th earl of Abercorn married Elizabeth, only daughter and heiress of Sir Robert Reading of Dublin.[5]

When resident in Strabane, the home of the Hamiltons was the castle. However, at different stages they lived elsewhere. It has already been mentioned that the 4th Lord Strabane was living at Feltrim in 1659 and it is probable that he continued to live here even after he was restored to his lands. His name does not appear in the hearth money roll of 1666 for Strabane and when he died in 1668 he was buried in Kenure Old Church, near Rush, Co. Dublin, where a monument erected by his widow survives. The 4th earl seems to have made Strabane his permanent home and strenuous efforts were made to have the 5th earl reside there. Writing to the bishop of Oxford in the summer of 1697, Bishop King described the earl as being of 'agreeable, easy and honourable conversation' and a 'good Protestant', and noted: 'The whole country, especially the gentry, seemed extremely taken with him and used all artifices to prevail upon him to settle on his Irish estate.'[6] King's sentiments towards the earl probably reflect more than a little of his relief that the head of the leading aristocratic family in his diocese had conformed. The 5th earl was preoccupied with problems elsewhere at this time. To clear off some of the debts on the manor of Strabane he and his wife had been forced to sell the greater part other jointure lands in Oxfordshire. He had also stood trial in Oxford in 1697 for the murder of John Prior of Burford, but had been acquitted.[7] An action which spoke clearly of his conformity as well as his interest in Strabane was his choosing to erect a seat for himself in the south aisle of the Anglican church in the town.[8] When he died at Strabane in June 1701 King was present with him.[9] There is no evidence that the 6th earl of Abercorn ever lived on his estate in Strabane barony. If he visited Strabane, he may have used the castle as a lodging, but essentially for the next century or so the Abercorns were absentee landlords.

Several members of the local gentry made Strabane their home, preferring to make the town their usual place of residence rather than live on their country estates. Those who belonged to this category included Oliver McCausland, Hugh Hamill and the McClenaghan family. The career of Oliver McCausland has already been considered. For him Strabane was the ideal location from which he could direct his many landed concerns. Though his principal landed interests were in neighbouring Co. Donegal, another of the more prominent residents of Strabane during this period was Hugh Hamill. His background is not clear, but he is likely to have been a member of a family which had connections with Strabane from the early 17th century.[10] The merchant, Patrick Hamilton senior, was married to a Hamill, and the witnesses to his will were Hugh Hamill, probably a name-sake rather than the man himself, and John Hamill. The latter was also witness to a deed in Strabane in 1665 and was a witness at an exchequer deposition in 1674 when his age was given as 65.[11] In the late 1670s Hugh Hamill bought the Lifford estate from the Hansards, one of the sureties for the purchase money being his brother-in-law, Abraham Creighton. In 1680 Hamill took out patents for markets and fairs at Ballindrait and Dunfanaghy in Co. Donegal and Castlederg in Co. Tyrone.[12] Ballindrait was a village on the Lifford estate, while Hamill also owned property in the Dunfanaghy area.[13] His relationship with Castlederg is not so clear and his acquisition of a patent for this village – around ten miles from Strabane – may have been speculative. As a prominent landowner in Donegal he twice served as high sheriff in 1682 and 1685.[14]

Hamill pursued an active, even aggressive, policy of buying up tenements and town parks in Strabane. It has already been noted in the previous chapter that this brought him into conflict with the 4th earl of Abercorn.[15] There is also evidence that he was involved in a property dispute with a fellow townsman, James Maghee, which did not go in Hamill's favour. In a memorandum drawn up by Hamill in 1685 he alleged to have 'quit' Maghee of his interest in Drumnaboy, a townland immediately south of Strabane, amounting he claimed to six barrels of oats per annum. However, as the following year Maghee conveyed his interest in Drumnaboy to Randal Brice and William Blachford, one can only conclude that Hamill's purchase was not recognized.[16] Hamill played a prominent role in the settler response to the Jacobite threat in the north-west in 1688–9. He was involved in the defence of Derry and was suffered a near fatal injury at the second battle of Windmill Hill. Subsequently he was heavily involved in the efforts to have the arrears of pay of the Derry garrison recovered. In 1692 he entered parliament as MP for the borough of Lifford. It is likely that Hamill overstretched himself with his many different concerns for when he died in 1709 he was heavily in debt.[17]

The McClenaghans were newcomers to the Strabane area and rose to prominence through military service in the 1640s. Andrew McClenaghan had served in the regiment of Lord Deputy Fleetwood.[18] He appears as the administrator of the estate of the late Cornet William McClenaghan – possibly his father or perhaps a brother – in a transaction involving property in Drogheda in 1671 and 1672.[19] He himself received lands in the barony of Dungannon as part of the Restoration land settlement.[20] The hearth money roll records two householders with this name in Strabane barony, one in Lisnaman (Newtownstewart) and the other in Strabane – it is possible that they were one and the same. A deed of May 1664 refers to the acquisition of property in the town of Strabane.[21] Andrew McClenaghan was involved in municipal government in Strabane, serving as provost of the town in 1675. Of undoubted benefit to the family was the alliance formed with the McCausland family. Andrew McClenaghan's son David married Margery, daughter of Alexander McCausland probably in the early 1670s. In 1678 David McClenaghan was granted the lands of Altaclady in the manor of Strabane in fee farm.[22] This was a large freehold of some 850 acres of generally good agricultural land and meant that the family now had a sound landed base in the barony. However, the principal residence of the family was in Strabane. McCausland, Hamill and the McClenaghans represent members of the gentry who lived in Strabane and had vested interests in the town. Others among the gentry of north-west Ulster had property in the town, but lived elsewhere. For example, the Leslies of Tyrkernaghan in Donagheady parish owned property in Strabane as did the Hamiltons of Ballyfatton.[23]

In economic terms the merchants were the most important grouping in Strabane. Socially they also exerted considerable influence. The lack of family papers or business records is an obstacle to understanding this community fully. Nonetheless enough has survived from will abstracts and deeds to allow to a partial insight into the lives of these merchants and their families. Several individuals and families stand out: John Moderwell, John Gamble and the Hamilton and Maxwell families. The Hamiltons had origins in Strabane barony prior to 1641. Patrick Hamilton was the fourth son of William Hamilton of Priestfield in Blantyre.[24] Along with his brother Hugh, the latter had come to Strabane barony in the early 17th century and settled at Ballyfatton which he was granted in fee farm in 1634. Patrick engaged in mercantile activities building up a profitable business. An indication of his success can be seen in the fact that some time before 1641 he and another man had loaned £700 to Sir William Stewart of Newtownstewart, while he had also acquired the townland of Dergalt near Strabane in fee farm.[25] In the 1650s he was involved in the rebuilding of Strabane.[26] Two of Patrick's sons, Patrick junior and James, continued the merchant business. The third son, Frederick, may also have done so; he died overseas prior to November 1669 when administration of his estate was granted to his brother James.[27]

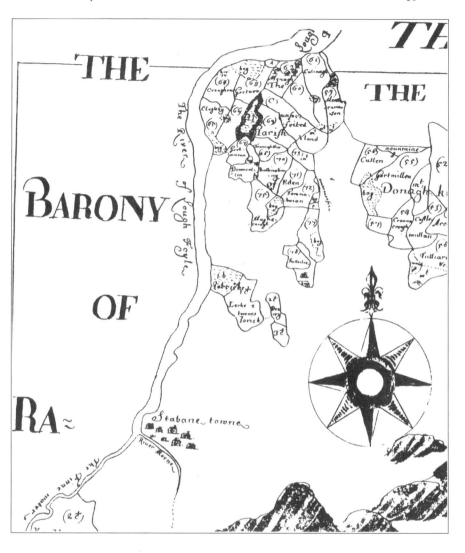

3 Strabane as represented on the Down Survey
map of Strabane barony, *c.*1657

The second of the two leading merchant families in Strabane was the Maxwell family. A deed of 1713 referring to John Maxwell's great-grandfather Arthur would suggest that the family had been resident in Strabane barony from the early 17th century. Thomas, William and James Maxwell appear as tax-payers in the 1666 hearth money roll for Strabane. It was Thomas who expanded the family's concerns with the acquisition of land. He was a prominent figure in local affairs and in 1681 served as high sheriff of Co. Tyrone. He was due to continue in this post for the following year as well until the intervention of the 4th earl of Abercorn who argued that this was too much of a burden for one solely dependent on trade for a living – not strictly true in Maxwell's case though. In his will of 1702 he appointed his sons to be his executors and to advise and assist them he named the Hon. Col. Gustavus Hamilton, Capt. David Creichton, David McClenaghan, John Love and John Douglas. Gustavus Hamilton was one of the most prominent figures in the north-west in this period. He was MP for Co. Donegal (and later of Strabane), and was one of the heroes of the Williamite War. He was also related to the Abercorns, being a nephew of the 1st earl. In 1686 and probably on other occasions he was part of the garrison stationed at Strabane which would have allowed him to have formed relationships within the local community.[28] In 1700 he registered a claim on the manor of Strabane with the trustees of the forfeited estates comprising four separate deeds totalling £953 plus interest made over a period between May 1697 and February 1698.[29]

The success of John Moderwell's merchant business can perhaps be best demonstrated by the fact that he was the only person living in Strabane in 1666 whose house contained three hearths.[30] His background is not clear, but the name Moderwell (or Motherwell) occurs on a number of occasions in the north-west in the early 17th century. A Robert Moderwell appears in the 1630 muster roll for the town of Strabane, while an Adam Moderwell of Donaghmore, Co. Donegal, died in 1632.[31] John Moderwell was the executor and possibly the son of Andrew Moderwell who received a lease of a barn and garden in Strabane from Captain Birsbane in 1654.[32] An indication of his local standing – and perhaps also of the power vacuum created by the forfeiture of the manor by the Catholic Lord Strabane – can be seen in the fact that he was returned to the General Convention of 1660 as the member for Strabane.[33] He was also one of the poll tax commissioners in 1661. His will, dated 16 March 1678 and proved 2 June 1679 mentions several tenements in the town of Strabane including one bought from a Mr Wallar (Mallar?) and another from a Mr Hamill.[34] He does not appear to have had any sons, but he left his daughters well provided for with Kathren and Jane each receiving £100 and Mary, 'being yet unportioned', £300. Geells Moderwell, perhaps his sister, is also mentioned in his will. One of Moderwell's tenements is mentioned in a deed of 1676 as situated on the south side of a shop granted to Patrick Hamilton junior.[35] Moderwell was a Presbyterian and represented the interests of the local congregation to the Laggan Presbytery.[36]

An insight into the business of one merchant is provided in the detailed abstract of the will and inventory of the aforementioned John Gamble.[37] Gamble is likely to have belonged to a family that had roots in Strabane for several generations. Probate of the will of John Leslie of Donagheady was issued to, among others, Robert Gamble Esq. in 1669 – it is significant that John Gamble appointed his 'kinsman' John Leslie of Tyrkernaghan in Donagheady parish an executor of his will – and a Robert Gamble was named on the Jacobite corporation of 1689.[38] Unlike many of the other merchants in Strabane, he was an Anglican and a correspondent of Bishop King of Derry. In 1701 Gamble expressed concerns to King about the presentation to Mevagh parish in Co. Donegal, of a Mr Nimmo, whom he considered untrustworthy.[39] He was appointed high sheriff of Co. Tyrone in 1707, but died during his year of office. In addition to his merchant business Gamble was the lessee of the bishop's lands in the parish of Leckpatrick for which he paid £10 rent and in the 1690s acquired at least four fee farm properties in or near Strabane.[40] His will was dated 9 April 1706 and was proved on 29 April 1707.

The will reveals that when Gamble drew up his will he had debts owed to him of £3,528. Gamble himself owed debts of £1,228, leaving a net estate of £2,400. His debtors included several of the gentry of north-west Ulster. The largest debt owed to him was £520 by the earl of Abercorn. Others who owed him substantial sums included Captain Mervyn (£116), Charles Hamilton of Cavan (Co. Donegal) (£220), Thomas Edwards Esq. (of Castlederg) (£120) and Alexander Montgomery (£306). £150 owed by a William Brown of London indicates trading links that went beyond Ulster and Scotland. Several smaller sums owed by a number of individuals who can be identified as merchants in Strabane and members of the lesser gentry are also listed. Among the merchandise owed to him were £240 in wine etc. in Derry with a Mr Anderson, £150 in brandy, salt and deals; £30 in livestock and £150 of 'book debts'. His partnership in a vessel, *The Margaret*, was valued at £200, while his leases and freeholds in Strabane and Leckpatrick were valued at £550. Of the sums owed by Gamble, the largest was £500 to 'Mr Cairns, Mr Conolly & bills'. He also owed his sister Mrs Dean £200 and Patrick Hamilton's children £50.

Gamble did not have a son when he wrote his will and he included a proviso that if a son was born he was to receive the leases and freeholds in Strabane and Leckpatrick. £40 was left to Thomas, son of Alderman Moncrieffe and Katherine Hamilton; if she died this was to go to the children of the late Patrick Hamilton of Strabane. Gamble's mother was still alive and she was left £5 a year. The value of Gamble's estate did not compare unfavourably with merchants elsewhere in Ulster, including Belfast.[41] He is likely to have been the wealthiest merchant in Strabane in this period, though comparisons with other merchants are hampered by the lack of similar documentation. If financial bequests alone are used, he was some way ahead of the other merchants. The only financial bequest mentioned in the 1702 will of Thomas Maxwell of Strabane was £80 to his grandson Arthur, though the fact that he had several landed properties to bequeath, probably mitigates this.[42] His son William left cash sums totalling £520 to his son-in-law and two unmarried daughters. Back in 1659 Patrick Hamilton senior had left financial bequests totalling £500 to four of his children. John Moderwell left the same amount to three of his daughters, including £300 to one daughter because she was 'yet unportioned'. Other Strabane merchants preferred – or perhaps through circumstances were forced to – bequeath houses, goods and personal effects to their spouses and offspring rather than cash sums.[43]

A will was an important means of securing the future well-being and livelihoods of the testator's family. His widow could be bequeathed a specific amount of money. She might also be left an annual sum arising from property to maintain her during her remaining years, though this was often on the basis that she did not remarry. John Gamble left his wife Jean £50 a year for the rest of her life, though this was to be reduced to £30 if she remarried. In his will of May 1659 Patrick Hamilton bequeathed to his 'dear and loving wife' £200 and his house and lands in Strabane during her lifetime.[44] Thomas Maxwell left his wife Mary one third of the free rents from Kirkminister, Co. Donegal, and his freehold of Knockroe in the manor of Strabane. He also gave her the room above the kitchen in his house in Strabane. Conscious that this could hinder the letting of the rest of the house, his instructed his sons to provide their mother with a large house in the town should this situation arise. John Moderwell left his wife the household furniture.[45] Bequests to unmarried daughters were designed to provide them with a dowry should a suitable marriage partner be found. John Gamble bequeathed his young daughters Jane, Anne and Sidney, respectively, £700, £600 and £500. Occasionally there were disputes over the disposal of the possessions and money of a deceased family member. The nuncupative will of Gabriel and Agnes Homes reveals that their son William 'having charge of his father's keys and knowing that there was concealed money' refused to give his sisters their share of their parents' estate.[46]

Wills also provide one of the few opportunities to peer into the material worlds of the merchant community of Strabane in this period. In the will of Gabriel and Agnes Homes of 1669, Agnes left her daughter Geiles her plaids and her woollen clothes with the exception of her best gown and petticoat which were to go to her other daughter Margaret; her linen clothes were to be divided equally between them. Their son William was left two pieces of new linen, two red rugs, three pairs of small linen sheets, half a dozen napkins and one third of all the pewter vessels in the house.[47] Thomas Maxwell left his son Richard a silver tankard and watch. Jointly with his mother Richard was also left six silver spoons, a silver tumbler, a silver salt and a silver taster. Thomas' daughter Rebecca was left twelve silver spoons and a silver fork. Similar items – possibly even the same – turn up in the will of Mary Maxwell, daughter of William and grand-daughter of Mary: a silver tankard was left to her nephew William Cairnes, a silver tumbler to her niece Jane Harvey, and one 'soupson', eight small spoons and two silver salts to her sister Rebecca.[48] In his will of 29 April 1703 James Hamilton of Strabane left his son James his silver hilted sword, his case of pistols and his saddle.[49] Such luxury items spoke of aspirations towards gentility. Because merchants could purchase goods at wholesale prices, it was possible for those with the means and inclination to acquire items beyond the reach of most.[50]

Not all bequests went to family members. Charitable bequests also feature in the testamentary papers of the merchant community. In 1659 Patrick Hamilton senior left £2 to the poor of the parish of Camus. John Gamble left £15 to the poor of Camus, and this was to be invested by the provost and minister. William and Mary Maxwell also left to the Camus poor the sums of, respectively, £8 and £5. Money could also be left to friends or those who were in the testator's employ or had shown them some kindness. Mary Maxwell left Widow Joanna Hamilton £6 for attending her during her sickness and James Lyon for his unspecified 'trouble'.

Strong bonds of kinship and friendship existed between these families. Intermarriage between the merchant families was fairly common. John Moderwell was a son-in-law of Patrick Hamilton senior. Moderwell appointed his brothers-in-law, Patrick and James Hamilton, along with Thomas Maxwell as the overseers of his estate.[51] James Hamilton appointed John Gamble one of his executors. Occasionally merchants looked beyond Strabane for marriage partners, either for themselves or their daughters. There was some intermarriage with the leading citizens of Derry. Katherine Hamilton, probably the daughter of Patrick Hamilton junior, was married to Alderman Thomas Moncreiffe, a leading figure in municipal government in that city who served as mayor on a number of occasions. He was very possibly related to David Moncreiffe who was one of the original burgesses in Strabane.[52] A daughter of Thomas Maxwell married Alderman Alexander Tomkins, another of the leading figures in Derry politics at this time, whose residence was at Prehen.[53] What is interesting about these marriages is that they crossed the religious divide and united Anglican and Presbyterian families, the non-conformists being from Strabane. Marriage settlements were a means of safeguarding the future of the bride should she outlive her husband and her surviving children. One that survives for Strabane concerns the intended marriage between John Maxwell, son of William, and Isabella, a

younger daughter of Patrick Hamilton of Omagh Esq.[54] Under the terms of
the marriage settlement, dated 24 March 1711, Maxwell's lands, comprising
the freehold of Knockroe and premises in Strabane, were vested with Patrick
Hamilton and the Revd William Read for the use of Isabella during her
widowhood. On the failure of her heirs the properties were to go to
Patrick's son, the Revd William Hamilton, then a curate in Templemore
parish and afterwards successively rector of Termonamongan and Camus-
juxta-Mourne parishes, and his heirs for sixty years.

     The wealth of the leading merchants did not entirely derive from their
business interests, but also from rural land-holdings. Land was both an
investment of the merchandising profits and an additional source of income.
Furthermore, it enhanced their social standing, elevating some families to
the status of gentry. Prior to 1641 Patrick Hamilton senior had acquired the
townland of Dergalt in fee farm. His son James acquired the lands of
Tullyard, Woodend and Roundhill, a fee farm in the manor of Cloghogall to
the north of Strabane. These lands had originally been granted to the Algeo
family, prominent as agents to the Hamiltons in the early 17th century, but
who disappear from the Strabane area in the late 1660s.[55] Thomas Maxwell
built up a considerable landed base in the latter part of the 17th century. In
May 1680 he purchased the former monastic lands of Kilfougher (or
Kirkminister) near Lifford in Co. Donegal for £700 from Thomas Grove of
Castleshanahan in that county.[56] Both Maxwell and James Hamilton took
advantage of the 5th earl of Abercorn's policy in the 1690s of granting large
swathes of the manor of Strabane in fee farm at a time when he was heavily
in debt. In 1698 James Hamilton was granted part of the quarterland of
Douglas in fee farm by the 5th earl of Abercorn, a massive holding of over
4,000 acres though much of it mountainous and of little agricultural value.[57]
In 1703 Hamilton bought these lands outright from the trustees of the
forfeited estates, via the Act for the Relief of Protestant Purchasers.[58]

     Thomas Maxwell was granted Knockroe in fee farm by the 5th earl of
Abercorn in 1695. As the owner of extended land-holdings, Maxwell was
able to leave his lands in Tyrone to his son William and those in Donegal to
his son Richard. In 1703 William Maxwell also took advantage of the Act for
the Relief of Protestant Purchasers to buy Knockroe from the trustees of the
forfeited estates, thus becoming the owner in fee simple of a small estate of
some 600 statute acres. In 1711 Knockroe together with some tenements in
Strabane provided William's son John with an annual income of £65. While
several merchants acquired small estates of their own, there is no evidence
that any merchant in Strabane gave up his business interests and retired to his
rural landholdings to live the life of a country gentleman. For some, the
ownership of land did occasionally mean that they were given the title of
gentleman, implying that they had risen in social status. Thomas Maxwell
was listed as a 'gent.' when he was among those attainted by James'

parliament in 1689, while his grandson John was styled 'gent.' in his marriage settlement in 1711.[59]

John Gamble's will reveals links with London. Several other members of Strabane merchant families were attracted to Dublin for the business opportunities it provided. Patrick Hamilton the younger was a merchant in Dublin when his father wrote his will in 1659, though he soon afterwards returned to Strabane.[60] Patrick Caldwell, son of Catherine Caldwell of Strabane, was a merchant in Dublin prior to 1720.[61] Higher education also provided the means to experience life outside of the north-west. Several Strabane inhabitants were able to send their sons to university. Some were sent to Dublin to be educated at Trinity College, including James Sinclair, son of the rector of Strabane, and Patrick and William McGhee, sons of the apothecary George.[62] Andrew, son of Patrick Hamilton jun., was at university, though probably in Scotland.[63] William Maxwell's son James was also educated in Scotland.[64] A few had experienced life much further afield. William Holmes, ordained Presbyterian minister in Strabane in 1692, had lived for a time in New England and returned there in 1714.[65]

A broad range of professions and trades were represented among the populace of the Strabane. While not enough information has survived to make possible a detailed breakdown of the occupational structure of the town, we can at least identify many of the tradesmen by name and the trade they followed. Weavers included William Ewart and William Kenlie.[66] Those involved in the production of luxury items included James Hector (or Ector) and Patrick Fleming, both glovers, and William Smelie, wigmaker.[67] Each would have catered for the needs of the wealthy in society and indicate a market for luxury goods. Such tradesmen were known in other Ulster towns in this period. In 1706 two wigmakers were admitted as freemen of the corporation of Derry.[68] John McMaster and Robert Baird were tailors.[69] Alexander Jamison was a baker in the 1670s and 1680s.[70] Shoemakers included Andrew Reid, John Hamilton, Thomas Urey and Bryce Boyd.[71] There is also mention of a carpenter, James Boyd, a blacksmith, James Knox, a glazier, John Cook, and a mason, William Loughridge.[72] Allan Cuthbert the elder was a tanner.[73]

Medical practitioners of various descriptions also resided in Strabane. These included the apothecaries, Robert Browne and George McGhee and the 'chirugeon', William Fleming.[74] The training for these professions was generally through apprenticeship. This could be through local tuition – in 1716 George McGhee had an apprentice named William Benson – or occasionally by sending the interested party to Britain for training there. In 1693 the Strabane merchant, John Love, travelled to Glasgow with brother-in-law, Alexander Herkes, to arrange with a surgeon there an apprenticeship for his nephew Thomas.[75] Because surgeons and apothecaries were usually not university educated they did not enjoy the same status as physicians, but

were deemed 'adept craftsmen'.[76] Nonetheless in contributing to local
health provision they provided an invaluable service to the communities
they served. The most prominent of them in Strabane was the aforementioned George McGhee, though this was not simply through his
apothecary business. He was a member of a family that had come to
Strabane barony from Scotland during the initial phase of the Plantation; his
grandfather David had been the agent to the Hamiltons for over 50 years.
McGhee played a leading role in local government in the town, serving as a
burgess on the Strabane corporation for over 40 years and in the 1730s being
heavily involved in the power struggle between the 6th earl of Abercorn and
the corporation.[77] He was married to Rebecca Hamilton, most probably a
daughter of Patrick Hamilton junior, and, if so, through her acquired the fee
farm of Dergalt in the manor of Strabane.[78] Strabane was not an assize town
and there is no evidence for a resident attorney in the town in this period.
Strabane was also home to clergymen, both Anglican and Presbyterian; these
individuals will be looked at in more detail in the next chapter.

4. The churches and religious controversy

The people of early modern Ireland were deeply religious and few viewed or understood their world without reference to God.[1] More than that, the way in which God should be worshipped, both publicly and privately was not simply a matter of conscience. Bound up with the notions of good governance and social order was the idea of an established church, one in which the interests of the state would be served to their mutual benefit. However, in Ireland only a minority of the populace shared this view. This chapter examines the churches in Strabane, institutionally and in terms of the relationship between the different denominations. Apart from a short-lived Quaker meeting in the town in the middle of the 17th century, the three main denominations in Strabane were the Church of Ireland, Presbyterian and Roman Catholic churches. In terms of numbers, the difficulties outlined above in relation to population figures also apply here. However, there are a few clues as to the relative numerical strength of the different denominations. In 1693 Bishop King reckoned the Church of Ireland population in the parish of Camus to be 100 persons, making it one of the larger Anglican congregations in the diocese of Derry, though considerably smaller than the Presbyterian population.[2] However, actual figures for the Presbyterian community are harder to come by. In 1695 Bishop King reckoned that there were 1,500 Presbyterians in the parish of Ardstraw to the south of Strabane, and as many as 5,000 when the number of non-conformists in neighbouring parishes was added to this figure.[3] The number of Catholics in Strabane was probably quite small if the hearth money returns are anything to go by when only three Irish families in the town paid hearth tax.

The basic unit in the Church of Ireland system was the parish and in the main the medieval network of parishes continued after the Reformation. Strabane lay within the bounds of the parish of Camus-juxta-Mourne, though at the northern end of it. In fact, as the Civil Survey noted, the churchyard bordered on the north the boundary between the parishes of Camus and Leckpatrick.[4] In the early 17th century the site of the parish church had been relocated to Strabane by the 1st earl of Abercorn. During the troubles of 1688–90 the Anglican churches in the north-west, like those in other parts of Ireland, suffered at the hands of Jacobite soldiers and their followers. The location of some of the buildings along the Foyle made them particularly vulnerable to Jacobite troops retreating from Derry after the siege. The church in Strabane had been damaged in the disturbances. It had also been used as a hospital by James' army; by the end of July 1689 there were reportedly 3,000 sick Jacobites at Strabane.[5] The communion utensils had been saved, however, and by the time of Bishop King's visitation in 1693 repairs had been carried out. Nothing at all survives of this church which was demolished when a new church was built a short distance away in the 1870s; it was one of the few churches in Ulster in this period which was cruciform in plan.[6]

From 1660 until 1703 the parish of Camus was held jointly with the neighbouring parish of Leckpatrick. The two parishes retained distinct identities, however, and there was considerable reluctance to amalgamate them, much of it stemming from concerns over the impact on the effective governance of the country. One objection raised in 1664 was the fact that it 'would create some trouble in the proceedings at assizes and sessions and the county would be less served with constables and churchwardens'. Another was the fear that the rector 'might presume himself able to serve both in one and the same place' and do without a curate which he was then obliged to employ.[7] The church in Camus was generally regarded as being the more important of the two, however, and this was reflected in the concerns that the rector should live in Strabane rather than in Leckpatrick. For example, in the visitation of 1693 it was noted that the rector did not live in Strabane, but about two miles away in Leckpatrick. The bishop recommended that the union of Camus and Leckpatrick ought to continue, but insisted that the rector should be obliged to live in Strabane where he was to have prayers read every day with a curate to assist him.

The officers of the parish in both civil and ecclesiastical matters were the churchwardens who were assisted by individuals known as sidesmen. Parish activities were financed by a parish levy or cess apploted on each townland. The men who collected the money from each townland were called apploters and they were appointed by the vestry. Other individuals were selected to oversee the work of the apploters. Of those who served as churchwardens in Strabane relatively little can be said. Robert Adams, who served as church-warden in 1686, was one of those from the settler community appointed to James II's corporation in 1688.[8] John Bunting, churchwarden in 1692–3, was a cordwainer who was the lessee in a deed involving several properties in Strabane in 1699.[9] A further parochial appointment was that of clerk. George Blewart was first recorded as parish clerk in 1693 and was still in this post in 1718. He had been parish clerk in Leckpatrick in 1686. He leased a few small-holdings from James Hamilton, merchant, immediately to the north of Strabane in the parish of Leckpatrick.[10]

Though few in number at local level, the Church of Ireland clergy formed an important social grouping and not simply as the representatives of the religious establishment. They also played an important role in local government, through parish vestries, and were often the eyes and ears of the authorities in Dublin and elsewhere. The first three rectors of the parish of Camus after 1660 were English born. Judging by the years in which they matriculated or graduated from university – in each case Cambridge – most were well into middle age.[11] The first, John Whitworth, came from Hertfordshire and was educated at Peterhouse College, Cambridge. He was followed by James Harwood and another native of Hertfordshire, Philip Johnson, both of whom were graduates of St John's College, Cambridge. Strabane was not unusual in this respect and in most parishes in the diocese of Derry in the immediate aftermath of the Restoration, the clerics were both English born and educated. Gradually, however, such men were replaced by ministers born in nearly every case on the island of Ireland. Instead of being graduates of Cambridge, most of these men were alumni of Trinity College, Dublin. A few were of Scottish background and one, John Sinclair, was rector of Camus from the late 1660s until his death in March 1703. According to one source, Sinclair was the son of James Sinclair of West Brimes in Caithness; his MA had probably been awarded by Glasgow University. Based on his age in an Exchequer deposition of 1672 was born about 1644.[12] He was ordained a deacon on 25 March 1664 and was ordained a priest six moths later serving initially as a curate in the parish of Urney. He was instituted to the parish of Leckpatrick in February 1666 and to Camus in February 1669. He was also rector of the parish of Tullyaughnish in the diocese of Raphoe from 1682.[13] He was held in high regard by his bishop, William King, and was one of King's allies in his campaign against non-conformists in Derry diocese.[14]

The Anglican clergy was far from a homogenous group, differing in background, wealth, taste and interests. Some invested in land, acquiring small estates through purchase or intermarriage with a landed family. Those who did so thereby entered the ranks of the gentry in their own right and not simply on the basis of family background. John Sinclair was one who invested in this way. In 1683 he purchased Holy Hill, a fee farm of over 2,000 acres in the manor of Cloghogall to the north of Strabane, from the McGhees. About 1685 the freehold of Holy Hill was reckoned to be worth nearly £30 a year, significantly augmenting Sinclair's income from his parishes which in 1694 was £100 a year.[15] He first wife is supposed to have been a Hamilton of the Abercorn connection, though this cannot be proved. He married secondly Anna, daughter of Lt Col. James Galbraith MP. Though marriage, therefore, Sinclair cemented his position among the local elite.[16]

Following Sinclair's death in 1703 David Jenkins, the former master of the diocesan school in Derry, was appointed to Camus, henceforth no longer united to Leckpatrick. Bishop King had previously intended appointing Jenkins, whom he considered popular and of good character to Urney parish, though in the event this did not happen.[17] Jenkins also sought to

acquire a landholding in the vicinity of Strabane and eyed the townland of
Magirr on the opposite side of the Mourne from Strabane. However, his
attempts to acquire this property were thwarted when the 6th earl of
Abercorn revealed that it had already been promised to another.[18] Jenkins
kept up a correspondence with Joshua Dawson, the under-secretary to the
chief secretary in Dublin, filling him in on items of news from Strabane and
the north-west and keeping him in tune with political developments and
intrigue. On the death of Queen Anne, Jenkins wrote to Dawson to express
his relief that 'a Protestant prince of the same Royal family fills the throne
and the Tories so unanimous in his Majesty's interest'.[19] Less is known of the
curates who served the parish of Camus during this period. While some
remained in this somewhat lowly position for all of their careers for other it
was simply a stepping stone to greater things. It was obviously helpful when
those in positions of influence were prepared to intervene on behalf of
aspiring clerics. John Campbell, earl of Breadalbane, wrote to King upon
hearing from Mr Young's wife of the bishop's kindness to the curate and
requesting King's support in recommending Young for promotion.[20]

The roots of Presbyterianism in the Strabane area go back to 1644 when
John Adamson, who was probably the son of Principal John Adamson of
Edinburgh University, was sent by the General Assembly of the Presbyterian
Church of Scotland to northwest Ulster. He subsequently became minister
of Leckpatrick and was the first clergyman based in this area who is known
to have held Presbyterian beliefs. During the Commonwealth period a
number of non-conformist clergymen served parishes in the Strabane area
and received their income either from the tithes of the parish or from a state
salary. In the town of Strabane Robert Brown ministered on an income of
£40 per annum which was later increased to £60. His successor was William
Keyes, previously minister of Raswell, Cheshire.[21] Conflict between those who
took differing positions on the nature of church government and religious
observance, was inevitable in an era where for many such things were
considered worth fighting and dying for. The year 1660 saw the restoration
not just of the monarchy, but also of the structures and episcopate of the
Church of Ireland. Those clergy who refused to recognize this were expelled
from the parishes they had hitherto served. The result was the beginning of a
clear separation of Presbyterianism and Anglicanism into two distinct
denominations.

The way in which the government and Church of Ireland hierarchy dealt
with the perceived threat from Protestant dissent varied. At times direct
action was taken against non-conformist ministers and their followers.
George Wild, bishop of Derry, was personally involved in efforts to counter
the activities of dissenters in his diocese in the years immediately after 1660.
In September 1661 he wrote to the archbishop of Armagh: 'Your Grace's
letter ... found me at Strabane, where I was forced to come for the preventing

[of] some great dangers which we justly feared from the notorious conventicles in those parts.'[22] The following March, Wild found the Presbyterians of Strabane more tractable: 'divers of them do court me already, and to prevent the indictments which I have threatened to put in tomorrow they have been all with me this day and promise conformity'.[23] The leaders of Presbyterianism continued to be targeted, however, and in August 1663 the Presbyterian minister in Strabane, Robert Wilson, along with a number of others, was arrested and imprisoned for a period.[24] In 1667 a large number of Presbyterians from the Strabane area were excommunicated by the bishop of Derry. According to the order for their expulsion, non-conformity was defined as 'not only absence from church, but baptising by unlicensed ministers'.[25]

Persecution was, however, intermittent and more governed by external factors and processes than by what was happening in Strabane itself. By the 1670s relations between the denominations were more relaxed and a meeting house was built in Strabane for the first time. However, specific events could bring the issue of Protestant dissent to the foreground once again and have reverberations which reached all parts of the kingdom. For example, when news of the Rye House conspiracies broke the earl of Arran ordered 'two troops of horse to march to Strabane ... that being the place inhabited by people much of the same stamp with those concerned in that detestable plot'.[26] The previous December Ezekiel Hopkins, bishop of Derry, had noted that the post office of Strabane was in the hands of 'persons who are zealous Presbyterians'.[27] Presbyterians were not the only Protestant dissenters in Strabane who faced opposition in this period. A Quaker meeting was established in Strabane in the late 1650s though no meeting house was ever erected. However, fears of persecution and the defection to the Church of Ireland of one of their leading members, Robert Burgess, who accepted the position of parish clerk, resulted in the disappearance of the Quaker presence in the town shortly after the Restoration.[28]

The supposed strength of the non-conformist interest in Strabane, as expressed in the fears of Hopkins and others, is difficult to square with the financial difficulties faced by the Presbyterian congregation in the town in the 1670s. In 1674 the Laggan presbytery found the congregation at Strabane negligent in their maintenance of Mr Wilson who was only paid £17 per annum. The following year Wilson complained to the presbytery of 'several grievances and difficulties which he finds in his work & labours at Strabane' and requested that the presbytery would 'declare him transportable'. His congregation stated that they could pay him no more than £25 per annum, and that was only because ten men paid most of it. There was even a request that the bounds of the Strabane congregation be extended to include 'half the parish of Leck[patrick], and that part of the parish of Ardstra which lies contiguous to them upon the east side of the river Morn may be stirred up to joyn with them'; it does not appear that this suggestion was carried through.[29] By July 1676 Wilson's position at Strabane had still not improved and so presbytery judged 'him not necessarily obliged to stay there'. However, his congregation were keen to retain his services and even promised to build him a meeting house. In October of that year Wilson agreed to stay on until at least the following May and it was reported to presbytery that he would 'stretch himself as far as he can to gratify them in their desire'. Wilson was in fact to remain at Strabane for a further thirteen years, dying in Derry in 1689 during the siege.[30] The situation at Strabane was by no means unique, however, with many congregations finding it difficult to give their ministers sufficient financial support.[31]

The parlous condition of the Presbyterian church in Strabane in the 1670s may in turn be a reflection of the financial position of the merchant community in the town at this time. Judging by the names of those who represented the congregation before the Laggan presbytery from 1672 to 1700 – John Moderwell, William Maxwell and James Hamilton to name but a few – merchants formed the leadership of Strabane's Presbyterian congregation.[32] In 1712 the six men appointed to act on behalf of the congregation in the conveyance of the site of the new meeting house were all described as merchants.[33] Support for the Presbyterian church could be expressed in a number of ways. Attendance at public worship and the celebration of the sacrament of the Lord's Supper were two expressions of sympathy with the denomination and its ministers. Another can be seen in the wills of William Maxwell and his daughter Mary both whom of whom left a cash bequest to William Holmes, the Presbyterian minister in Strabane.[34] The closeness of the relationship between Holmes and his flock can be seen in the fact that he was appointed an overseer in the wills of Thomas Wilson (1693) and James Hamilton (1703).[35]

Opposition to the activities of Presbyterians might be directed at an institutional level, but the role of individuals was crucial if any impact was to be felt in the localities. The MP for Strabane, Oliver McCausland, was an inveterate opponent of Presbyterianism. When plans to introduce a Presbyterian minister to Stranorlar parish were discovered in 1708, William King, by this time archbishop of Dublin, encouraged McCausland to take action.[36] McCausland's earlier opposition in 1695 to the request of the Presbyterians of Ardstraw to build a meeting house on bishopric land in the parish seems to have been partly based on a personal animosity towards the Presbyterian minister, Samuel Halyday, and he declared his 'resolve not to suffer such a man to teach the people'. McCausland's attitude towards the unorthodox expression of religion is revealed in a strange episode concerning a 36-year-old woman named Jane Hodge from the parish of Ardstraw who fasted for three months and did not speak during that time. The case fascinated McCausland who wrote at length on it to Viscount

Mountjoy in the autumn of 1685 who in turn brought it to the attention of the Dublin Philosophical Society. When Hodge began her eccentric behaviour McCausland visited her often; advice was taken from doctors, including one by the name of Gray who advised that she be stripped and whipped if she did not speak. At one point she was put into a 'vast house' and there was warned by McCausland and another man that if she did not speak they would burn her. This did not have any effect and so they placed her hands on burning coals and threatened to ram heated tongs down her throat. She responded by throwing part of the fire back at them. They then took her to Ardstraw and hung her over the side of the bridge, but still this did not force her to break her silence. Eventually she accepted some meat from Captain Thomas Stewart. She then asked to be taken to Newtownstewart where she proclaimed that she had fasted 'for the sins of the people' and that she was the 'saviour of the nations'. McCausland believed that she sympathized with Presbyterianism.[37]

The political tensions between conformists and dissenters in Strabane are revealed in the attempts of the Revd John Sinclair to have David McClenaghan barred from the office of provost of the town. In June 1700 Sinclair revealed his concerns in this matter to Bishop King.[38] McClenaghan had been provost continuously since the end of the Williamite war and this alone was a 'good reason he should not be longer'. However, Sinclair feared that a 'strong party of Presbyterians' would again elect him as provost. Reminding King 'what a scandalous ill man he is in his morals', he pointed out that McClenaghan actively discouraged people from attending the parish church and requested the bishop's assistance to prevent him from being elected. This was not the first time that McClenaghan had incurred the wrath of the Anglican establishment. Previously he had prevaricated over the construction of a seat in the parish church for the provost of burgesses and in both November 1696 and January 1698 Bishop King had written to McClenaghan to implore him to repent of his sins, presumably referring to his non-conformity.[39] Whether or not Sinclair had his way on this occasion is not clear. His antipathy to non-conformity was palpable. In recommending a neighbouring curate for promotion, he pointed out that the man had held his ground against 'the faction' wherever he had been posted and had added to the number of conformists in his parishes.[40] In spite of these controversies, on a day-to-day basis relations between Presbyterians and Anglicans in Strabane seem for the most part to have been good. In his will William Maxwell, one of the leading Presbyterian merchants in Strabane, could refer to Oliver McCausland as 'my dear brother'.[41] The 6th earl of Abercorn was himself considered to be sympathetic to Presbyterians.[42]

Of the workings of the Roman Catholic church in Strabane in this period, very little at all can be said. In 1694 Fergus Lea was appointed bishop of Derry, the first such appointment in the diocese for over one hundred years. However, the administration of ecclesiastical affairs in the diocese for most of this period was in the hands of the vicar apostolic, Bernard O'Kane.[43] As with Presbyterian ministers, there were periods in which the Catholic clergy were persecuted. In late 1696 five priests, including Teig O'Linsechan, priest in Leckpatrick parish, were arrested by the high sheriff of Co. Tyrone and imprisoned in Strabane for at least four weeks, though where exactly they were incarcerated is not known.[44] The relationship between the Catholic clergy and settler community was not entirely one of hostility. In 1704 the aforementioned Teig O'Linsechan, was described as a 'man of peacable and inoffensive behaviour, well-beloved by his Protestant neighbours'.[45] The priest in Camus parish at this time was James O'Devin who lived at Bernagh. He was born around 1656 and had received his orders at Ballyna, Co. Kildare, in 1680.[46] Of his life and career nothing else is known. However, it is worth pointing out that his place of residence, Bernagh, or Bearney, was actually glebe land held by the Church of Ireland rector of Camus, at this time David Jenkins. That he was permitted to live here at all is an indication of a certain amount of toleration by the Anglican establishment. There does not appear to have been a mass-house in the vicinity of Strabane prior to the death of Queen Anne, though a deed of 1729 refers to 'mass-house meadow' suggesting that by this time a place of public worship had been erected near the town.[47]

An interesting change from the first half of the 17th century was the disappearance of a Catholic element among the leading members of the settler community. Prior to 1641, and under the patronage of the Catholic Hamilton landlords in the Strabane area, a small but significant number of Catholic Scots had settled in north-west Tyrone. Some were in positions of considerable influence and authority. Robert Algeo and David McGhee were successively agents to Sir George Hamilton of Greenlaw.[48] McGhee in particular was a prominent figure. However, by the end of the 17th century the Algeo family had disappeared from the district, while the McGhees had conformed. One can only speculate on the reasons for this, but clearly the religious latitude which had survived more or less to the Williamite period no longer existed from the 1690s.

In this period educational provision was closely bound up with religious reform. Because of this it frequently became a source of contention between the competing denominations. The Act of Uniformity of 1665 forbade schoolmasters from teaching unless they had been issued with a license by the Church of Ireland. There were a number of schools in Strabane in this period maintained by the churches. Not all the teachers were acceptable to the townspeople. One who failed to satisfy the inhabitants of the town was a Mr Paton who 'by reason of his incapability was turned out by the townsmen' in 1665.[49] He was offered alternative employment as a curate in one of the parishes in Derry diocese. When the bishop was informed of this by Major Perkins of Lifford he felt his judgment was under examination and responded by telling Perkins that he 'need not have jeered and lashed' at him. He claimed ignorance of the situation and pointed out that 'it was upon the town of Strabane's desires' that he had licensed Paton.[50] Other schoolmasters were a cause of concern to the authorities on account of their religious beliefs. In 1673 it was brought to the attention of James Margetson, archbishop of Armagh, that there was a school in Strabane 'taught by a ffanaticke person, which tends to the further perverting of the people'.[51] Teaching could provide an additional source of income for curates. In the 1680s Daniel Magee combined the duties of curate with those of school-master in Strabane.[52] In 1695 Bishop King did not think it was necessary to have a Latin school in Strabane, but believed that Mr Robertson, the curate, would make for an able schoolmaster and would do it for reasonable pay.[53] In 1714 the 6th earl of Abercorn turned his attention to the educational needs of the town when he founded a school in Strabane and endowed it £32 per annum out of lands at Ballysinode, part of his estate in Co. Tipperary. The rectors of Taughboyne, Donagheady and Camus and the provost of Strabane were to be its perpetual trustees.[54] It was probably at this school that Mr Ballentine taught; several of his pupils went on to study at Trinity College, Dublin.[55]

Conclusion

The 18th century saw Strabane develop into one of the most important economic centres in Ulster. This study has focussed on an earlier period in the town's history. It has not had the benefit of one large collection of documentary material to draw on. Rather it has sought to piece together a range of disparate sources in order to reconstruct the urban community of an Irish town and the physical world within which it operated. Many questions remain unanswered and much of the information that has been assembled here allows for only tentative conclusions on certain aspects of life and work in the town. We still know very little about how the town functioned both socially and economically. Certainly we have been able to identify the main players, those who were the prime movers and shakers in the town, but most aspects of their everyday lives remain hidden. In reviewing the changes that occurred in Strabane in the period covered by this study it is useful to pose the question: what were the main differences between the town of 1660 and that of 1714?

First of all, there was a major difference at a proprietorial level. In 1660 there was considerable uncertainty over who actually owned the town and manor of Strabane. Because of their support for the Royalist cause Strabane had been forfeited by the Hamiltons and was granted to a leading Cromwellian official in Ireland in the late 1650s. In 1659 Lord Strabane was an impoverished exile living in north Co. Dublin. However, at the Restoration the Hamiltons again found favour and Lord Strabane was restored to his estates. Strabane was the most important town in Ireland in this period with a resident proprietor of British Catholic background. The family's support for the Jacobite cause resulted in the forfeiture of their lands for a second time in the early 1690s. There followed the complexities of the Williamite land settlement before another member of the family, the 6th earl of Abercorn, purchased the town and manor of Strabane and added them to his already extensive estate in north-west Ulster. Thus by 1714 the question of who owned Strabane had been settled and the proprietorial insecurities which had been a feature of the seventeenth century were resolved.

The physical changes to the town in this period are harder to trace. The absence of a map or a detailed survey means that it is difficult to plot the layout of the town in this period with any assurance. However, the evidence suggests that the present Main Street in Strabane was the main area of economic activity in the town in this period. The most important building in the town for most of the 17th century was the castle built by the Hamiltons. However, by the end of this period it was no longer occupied, certainly not by the town's proprietor. By the 1670s the establishment of a Presbyterian congregation in Strabane created a need for a second place of public worship in the town, rivalling the Church of Ireland church as the primary focus for the communal expression of faith. By the late 1670s there was a further public building in the town in the form of a market house.

Economically Strabane in 1660 was only just beginning to recover from the dislocation caused by the upheavals of the 1640s and early 1650s. Its economic basis at this time was primarily agricultural with the town's weekly market serving as an outlet for the distribution of surplus farming produce. However, by the second decade of the eighteenth century the linen industry had been firmly established in the Strabane area and was trans-forming economic life in the town. As a result Strabane became one of the leading trading centres in the north of Ireland. Those who were involved in commercial activity were drawn from a relatively small and tightly knit community. The evidence suggests that most of them were drawn from families that had already been established in Strabane in the period before 1641. The degree of continuity from the first half of the seventeenth century to the second was an important feature in the development of early modern Strabane. A major reason for this was the fact that in the early 17th century a colony of Scots with secure property rights had been established in the town. The liberal use of fee farm grants had created a propertied class secure in their holdings. Their fee farm tenements could be sold or mortgaged and used as a means of raising revenue which in turn could be invested in schemes to develop the local economy. This combined with support from the town's proprietor, the 6th earl of Abercorn, and developments in the Irish economy in general, resulted in Strabane emerging as one of the more significant provincial towns in 18th-century Ireland.

Notes

ABBREVIATIONS

BL   British Library
CSPI   *Calendar of the State Papers relating to Ireland, 1509–1670* (24 vols, London, 1860–1912)
HMC   Historical Manuscripts Commission
Inq. Ult.   *Inquisitionum in officio rotolurum cancellariae Hiberniae asservatarum repertorium, Ultonia* (Dublin, 1827)
NAI   National Archives of Ireland
NLI   National Library of Ireland
TCD   Trinity College, Dublin, Manuscripts Room
PRONI   Public Record Office of Northern Ireland
RCBL   Representative Church Body Library
RDD   Registry of Deeds, Dublin

INTRODUCTION

1 R. Gillespie, 'The world of Andrew Rowan: economy and society in Restoration Antrim' in B. Collins, P. Ollerenshaw & T. Parkhill (eds), *Industry, trade and people in Ireland, 1650–1950: essays in honour of W.H. Crawford* (Belfast, 2005), p. 10.

2 G. Camblin, *The town in Ulster* (Belfast, 1951), pp 17–46; R.J. Hunter, 'Towns in the Ulster Plantation' in *Studia Hibernica* xi (1971), pp 40–79; R.J. Hunter, 'Ulster Plantation towns, 1609–41' in D.W. Harkness and M. O'Dowd (eds), *The town in Ireland: Historical Studies XIII* (Belfast, 1981), pp 55–80; R. Gillespie, 'The origins and development of an Ulster urban network', *Irish Historical Studies*, xxiv, 93 (1984), pp 15–29.

3 R. Gillespie, 'The small towns of Ulster, 1600–1700' in *Ulster Folklife* 36 (1990), pp 23–31; R. Gillespie, 'Small towns in early modern Ireland' in P. Clark (ed.), *Small towns in early modern Europe* (Cambridge, 1995), pp 148–65.

4 T.C. Barnard, 'The cultures of eighteenth-century Irish towns' in P. Borsay and L. Proudfoot (eds), *Provincial towns in early modern England and Ireland.*

Change, convergence and divergence (Oxford, 1992), pp 195–222; see also his extensive coverage of urban society and culture in *A new anatomy of Ireland: the Irish Protestants, 1649–1770* (New Haven and London, 2003) and *Making the grand Figure: lives and possessions in Ireland, 1641–1770* (New Haven and London, 2004).

5 J. Agnew, *Belfast merchant families in the seventeenth century* (Dublin, 1997).

6 B. O Dalaigh, *Ennis in the 18th century: portrait of an urban community* (Dublin, 1995); T. King, *Carlow: manor and town, 1674–1721* (Dublin, 1997).

7 PRONI, D/623, especially the B subsection.

8 PRONI, D/1854/2.

9 TCD, MS 1995–2008 and 750.

10 R.J. Hunter (ed.), *The plantation in Ulster in Strabane barony, Co. Tyrone, c.1600–41* (Coleraine, Institute of Continuing Education, New University of Ulster, 1982).

11 J.M. Cox, 'The Plantation and seventeenth-century developments', pp 57–80; J. Dooher, 'The development of Strabane in the eighteenth century', pp 81–96; W.J. Roulston, 'Strabane Presbyterianism', pp 298–313, all in

J. Bradley et al., *The fair river valley: Strabane through the ages*, ed. J. Dooher and M. Kennedy (Belfast, 2000).

12 A.P.W. Malcomson, 'The politics of "natural right": the Abercorn family and Strabane borough' in G.A Hayes-McCoy (ed.), *Historical Studies*, x (Galway, 1976), pp 43–81.

13 W.J. Roulston, 'The evolution of the Abercorn estate in north-west Ulster, 1610–1703' in *Familia* 15 (1999), pp 54–67; W.J. Roulston, 'Seventeenth-century manors in the barony of Strabane' in J. Lyttleton and T. O'Keeffe (eds), *The manor in medieval and early modern Ireland* (Dublin, 2005), pp 160–87.

1. LANDLORD AND CORPORATION

1 More in-depth studies are Roulston, 'Evolution of the Abercorn estate' and Roulston, 'Seventeenth-century manors in the barony of Strabane'.
2 *CSPI, 1633–47*, p. 53.
3 *Inq. Ult.*, 1 *Tempore Interregni*.
4 R. Dunlop, *Ireland under the Commonwealth* (2 vols, Manchester, 1913), ii, 650; S. Pender (ed.), *A census of Ireland, circa 1659* (Dublin, 1939), p. 388.
5 *CSPI, 1647–60*, p. 628.
6 Bodleian Library, Oxford, Carte MS 41, fo. 648, 42, 210.
7 W.R. Young, *Fighters of Derry* (London, 1932), p. 265.
8 R. Doherty, *The Williamite War in Ireland, 1688–91* (Dublin, 1998), p. 183.
9 PRONI, D/623/B/4/38, 39.
10 TCD, MS 750/2/3/14–5, William King to Robert Huntington, bishop of Raphoe, 24 June 1701; TNA (London) PROB/11/477.
11 Shropshire Record Office, MS 112/1/1661, Lord Rochester to the Hon. Richard Hill, 23 Sept. 1701.
12 PRONI, D/1854/2/15, Commissions, orders etc. book 7, pp 77–8.
13 PRONI, D/1854/2/29a.
14 G. Hamilton, *A history of the house of Hamilton* (Edinburgh, 1933), p. 43.
15 Hunter, *The Plantation in Ulster in Strabane barony*, p. 33; E.M. Johnston-Liik, *History of the Irish parliament, 1692–1800* (6 vols, Belfast, 2002), ii, 337.
16 Hamilton, *House of Hamilton*, p. 1027; BL, Add. MS 1778; RDD, 40.136.24649.

17 HMC *14th Report, Ormonde MSS*, i, p. 295.
18 RDD, 4.460.1160; 15.277.7489.
19 J. Graham, *Derriana* (Londonderry, 1823), p. 43.
20 J.G. Simms, 'Irish Jacobites: lists from TCD, MS N.1.3' in *Analecta Hibernica* 22 (1960), p. 60.
21 PRONI, D/546/2.
22 Abstract of title of Holy Hill (private possession).
23 J. Hanly (ed.), *The letters of Saint Oliver Plunkett, 1625–81* (Dublin, 1979), p. 546, no. 207, Plunkett to Tanari, 19 June 1680.
24 Simms, 'Irish Jacobites', p. 59.
25 Young, *Fighters of Derry*, pp 277–8; E. Berwick (ed.), *The Rawdon papers* (London, 1819), p. 360; K. Newman, *Dictionary of Ulster biography* (Belfast, 1993), p. 208.
26 TCD, MS 1995–2008/772, Captain [Oliver] McCausland to William King, 6 March 1700–1.
27 PRONI, T/808/7467.
28 PRONI, D/623/A/5/1, Robert Patterson to the Hon. James Hamilton, 13 July 1732; D/623/A/5/4, George McGhee to Lord Paisley, 5 Sept. 1732.
29 D.W. Hayton, 'Exclusion, conformity and parliamentary representation: the impact of the sacramental test on Irish dissenting politics' in K. Herlihy (ed.), *The politics of Irish dissent, 1650–1800* (Dublin, 1997), pp 64–5; Agnew, *Belfast merchant families*, pp 94–7.
30 TCD, MS 1995–2008/766, Dean Bolton to William King, 10 Dec. 1700; /777, same to same, 22 March 1700–01.
31 PRONI, D/669/17; NAI, Lodge MSS, viii, p. 244; *Reports from the Commissioners appointed … respecting the Public Records of Ireland* (London, 1825), p. 629.
32 Young, *Fighters of Derry*, pp 106–7, quoting from Burke's *Landed gentry of Ireland* (1904 edition).
33 PRONI, T/609/1. The date is 6 December 171[?], the last digit being illegible.
34 PRONI, D/669/29A-D.
35 Johnston-Liik, *History of the Irish parliament*, v, 164–5.
36 PRONI, MIC/600/5.
37 PRONI, D/669/19.
38 PRONI, T/2825/C/39/1–18.
39 W. H. Crawford, 'The evolution of the urban network' in W. Nolan, L. Ronayne and M. Dunlevy (eds), *Donegal: history and society* (Dublin, 1995), p. 388.

40 PRONI, D/683/286, rental of the bishopric of Derry, 1718 (possibly quoting from an earlier rental).

41 TCD, 1995–2008/1120, Abercorn to King, 20 Oct. 1704.

42 Malcomson, 'Politics of "natural right"', pp 46–7.

43 HMC *14th Report, Ormonde MSS*, i, p. 54.

2. POPULATION, TOPOGRAPHY AND ECONOMY

1 G. Hill, *An historical account of the plantation of Ulster at the commencement of the seventeenth century* (Belfast, 1877), p. 527.

2 PRONI, T/2941/1, Francis Vaughan et al. to earl of Ormonde, 6 Apr. 1641.

3 R.C. Simington (ed.), *The Civil Survey III, counties Donegal, Londonderry and Tyrone* (Dublin, 1937), p. 373.

4 PRONI, D/1062/4/3/3.

5 PRONI, D/1939/18/10/2.

6 PRONI, T/808/898.

7 Bodleian Library, Oxford, Carte MS 30, fo. 583.

8 W.J. Roulston, 'The Ulster Plantation in the manor of Dunnalong, 1610–70' in H. Jefferies and C. Dillon (eds), *Tyrone: history and society* (Dublin, 2000), p. 283.

9 S.T. Carleton, *Heads and hearths: the hearth money rolls and poll tax returns for Co. Antrim, 1660–69* (Belfast, 1991), pp 177–8.

10 *Journal of the house of commons of Ireland*, ii, 2nd pt, appendix, p. xxxviii.

11 This calculation is based on Raymond Gillespie's methodology for estimating the population of the barony of O'Neilland in Co. Armagh (R. Gillespie, *Settlement and survival on an Ulster estate,* Belfast, 1988, p. xvi).

12 Gillespie, *Settlement and survival*, p. xvi.

13 W. Macafee and V. Morgan, 'Population in Ulster, 1660–1760' in P. Roebuck (ed.), *Plantation to Partition: essays in Ulster history in honour of J.L. McCracken* (Belfast, 1981), pp 57–8.

14 PRONI, T/307A.

15 Roulston, 'Seventeenth century manors in the barony of Strabane', pp 164, 180–1.

16 Simington (ed.), *Civil Survey III*, p. 373.

17 In hearth money roll as Lisnaman.

18 PRONI, D/623/B/13/12.

19 TCD, MS 883/2, p.148.

20 *Inq. Ult.*, 10 Carolus I.

21 PRONI, T/307A.

22 Gillespie, 'Small towns of early modern Ireland', p. 153.

23 PRONI, T/505/1.

24 Johnston-Liik, *History of the Irish parliament*, ii, 339.

25 F.G. James, 'Derry in the time of George I: selections from Bishop Nicolson's letters, 1718–22' in *Ulster Journal of Archaeology*, 3rd series 17 (1954), p. 176; D.W. Hayton (ed.), *Letters of Marmaduke Coghill, 1722–1738* (Dublin, 2005), p. 11, n. 32; A. Dyer, 'Small towns in England' in P. Borsay and L. Proudfoot (eds), *Provincial towns in early modern England and Ireland: change, convergence and divergence* (Oxford, 1992), pp 53–67.

26 PRONI, T/307A.

27 Dunlop, *Ireland under the Commonwealth*, i, 666.

28 PRONI, T/558/8; D/1386/11.

29 J. Lodge, *The peerage of Ireland*, revised, enlarged and continued to the present time by Mervyn Archdall (7 vols, London, 1789), v, 114; J. Graham, *Derriana* (Londonderry, 1823), p. 35; Simington (ed.), *Civil Survey III*, pp 373, 391; TCD, MS 750/2/3/14–15.

30 PRONI, D/623/B/3/6.

31 This meeting house may have been standing from as far back as September 1693 when it was reported to the Laggan presbytery that a new church building would be finished in Strabane within the next two weeks (PRONI, MIC/637/6); RDD, 10.161.3309.

32 PRONI, D/1062/3/9.

33 PRONI, D/1062/3/15; RDD, 4.460.1160, 11.370.4758.

34 TCD, MS 1995–2008/149, Revd John Andrews to William King, 9 July 1691.

35 NLI, MS 8014/viii.

36 Simington (ed.), *Civil Survey III*, p. 391.

37 T.W. Moody, 'The revised articles of the Ulster Plantation' in *Bulletin of the Institute of Historical Research*, 12 (1934–5), p. 181; for a detailed consideration of fee farm grants see J.C.W. Wylie, *Irish land law* (London, 1975), pp 171–97.

38 R.A. Dodgshon, *Land and society in early Scotland* (Oxford, 1981), pp 101–2; K. Wrightson, *Earthly necessities: economic lives in early modern Britain, 1470–1750* (London, 2002), pp 72–3.

39 PRONI, LPC/771; *A list of the claims as they are entered with the trustees at*

Chichester House on College Green, Dublin, on or before the tenth of August 1700 (Dublin, 1701), pp 347–53.

40 HMC *14th Report, Ormonde MSS*, i, 54.

41 *A list of the claims*, pp 347–53.

42 PRONI, D/1386/11.

43 Gillespie, *Settlement and survival*, pp xl, liii.

44 Gillespie, 'The world of Andrew Rowan', pp 20–1.

45 PRONI, D/2977/3A/4/65/2–25.

46 E. Hamilton, *The Hamilton memoirs* (Dundalk, 1920), p. 4; PRONI, D/1939/18/10/2.

47 PRONI, T/808/898.

48 PRONI, D/1118/3/9/1.

49 PRONI, D/1939/18/10/2, 'Observations of H. Hamill Esq.'s title and interest in the lordship of Strabane', *c.*1685.

50 PRONI, D/1939/18/10/2.

51 PRONI, T/1365/1

52 PRONI, D/623/B/13/5

53 Simington (ed.), *Civil Survey III*, p. 392.

54 PRONI, LPC/1323.

55 PRONI, D/1854/2/5, fo. 48.

56 PRONI, D/1854/2/29a.

57 Gillespie, *Settlement and society*, p. xli.

58 PRONI, D/623/C/4/1, rental of the manor of Strabane, 1794–1809.

59 Gillespie, Settlement and survival, p. xl.

60 PRONI, D/1062/3/15.

61 *Reports of the Commissioners … Public Records of Ireland*, p. 379.

62 TCD, MS 750/1/76, William King to 5th earl of Abercorn, 8 June 1697. The recent recovery of some timbers from the river Mourne which have been dendro-dated to the late 1690s are possibly from this bridge and deserve further investigation.

63 PRONI, D/623/B/13/8.

64 RDD, 12.316.5237.

65 Roulston, 'Ulster Plantation in the manor of Dunnalong', pp 276–7; PRONI, T/544/1.

66 PRONI, D/1939/18/10/3.

67 PRONI, D/1062/3/11.

68 Simms, 'Irish Jacobites', p. 60.

69 PRONI, D/1062/4/B.

70 T. W. Moody and J. G. Simms (eds), *The bishopric of Derry and the Irish Society of London, 1602–1705* (2 vols, Dublin, 1968–83), ii, 174.

71 R. Gillespie, *The transformation of the Irish economy* (Dundalk, 1991), pp 44–7; R. Gillespie, *Seventeenth-century Ireland* (Dublin, 2006), pp 248–51.

72 G. Kirkham, 'Economic diversification in a marginal economy: a case study' in P.

Roebuck (ed.), *Plantation to Partition*. p. 64; G. Kirkham, '"To pay the rent and lay up riches": economic opportunity in eighteenth-century north-west Ulster' in R. Mitchison and P. Roebuck (eds), *Economy and society in Scotland and Ireland, 1500–1939* (Edinburgh, 1988), pp 95–104.

73 Hunter, *Plantation of Ulster in Strabane barony*, pp 27–39; *Report of commissioners appointed to inquire into the state of fairs and markets in Ireland*, HC 1852–3 (1674), xli, pp 57, 111.

74 PRONI, D/888/1.

75 Pender, *Census of Ireland*, p. 53.

76 C. S. King (ed.), *A great archbishop of Dublin: William King DD, 1650–1729* (London, 1906), pp 31–2.

77 Agnew, *Belfast merchant families*.

78 P. Seaby, *Coins and tokens of Ireland* (London, 1970), p. 134.

79 Gillespie, 'The world of Andrew Rowan', p. 23.

80 Gillespie, 'Small towns in early modern Ireland', p. 164. The lack of a detailed study of society and economy in the city of Derry in this period is one of the most significant gaps in the historiography of urban settlement in Ireland. An important resource which provides a cartographic basis for the further study of the city is A. Thomas, *Irish Historic Towns Atlas No. 15: Derry–Londonderry* (Dublin, 2005).

81 PRONI, LA/79/2AA/3B, pp 24–5, 27.

82 *Journal of the house of commons of Ireland*, ii, pt i, p. 473.

83 PRONI, LA/79/2AA/3B, pp 29–30.

84 PRONI, T/808/991; Simington (ed.), *Civil Survey III*, p. 394.

85 Simington (ed.), *Civil Survey III*, p. 373.

86 PRONI, D/1854/2/29a.

87 NAI, M2533.

88 Hunter, 'Ulster Plantation towns', p. 73.

89 W. H. Crawford, 'The origins of the linen industry in north Armagh and the Lagan valley' in *Ulster Folklife* 17 (1971), pp 42–51.

90 PRONI, D/623/A/2/1.

91 PRONI, T/581/3, p. 192; *Journal of the Association for the Preservations of Memorials of the Dead in Ireland*, 12, p. 295; gravestone in Clogher cathedral churchyard.

92 'Hollowa' may be a misreading of Holland, the name applied to a finely woven, strong cloth; 'mushlan' is presumably muslin, a cotton fabric first

made in India; 'tickin' is ticking, a linen twill: B. Collins and P. Ollerenshaw (eds), *The European linen industry in historical perspective* (Oxford, 2003), pp xxiii, xxv.

93 Gillespie, *Settlement and survival*, p. xxxix.

94 TCD, MS 883/2.

95 Gillespie, *Settlement and survival*, p. xxxvi; W.H. Crawford, *The impact of the domestic linen industry in Ulster* (Belfast, 2005), p. 62.

96 *Precedents and abstracts from the journals of the Trustees of the linen and hempen manufactures of Ireland* (Dublin, 1784), p. 2.

97 PRONI, D/623/A/5/10, 6th earl of Abercorn to Mr Nisbitt, 15 Jan. 1732–3.

98 TCD, MS 1995–2008/945, Capt. John Henderson to William King, 2 Oct. 1702.

99 RDD, 2.16.218; *Journal of the Irish house of commons*, ii, 2nd pt, p. cci.

1 PRONI, D/1854/2/8, Register's minute book no. 1, p. 73; NAI, M2533; TCD, MS 1995–2008/2356.

2 Crawford, *Impact of the domestic linen industry*, p. 63.

3. URBAN SOCIETY

1 Barnard, *A new anatomy of Ireland*; Barnard, *Making the grand figure*; D. Dickson, *Old World colony: Cork and south Munster, 1630–1830* (Cork, 2005); Maighread Ni Mhurchadha, *Fingal, 1603–60: contending neighbours in north Dublin* (Dublin, 2005).

2 Pender (ed.), *Census of Ireland*, p. 627.

3 C. Lennon, *The lords of Dublin in the age of Reformation* (Dublin, 1989), pp 246–7; Pender (ed.), *A census of Ireland*, p. 388.

4 HMC *Ormonde MSS*, n.s., vi, p. 486.

5 Hamilton, *House of Hamilton*, p. 44.

6 TCD, MS 750/1/77, William King to John Hough, bishop of Oxford, 8 June 1697.

7 PRONI, D/623/B/4/44; *The Complete Peerage*, i, 5; Nottingham University Library, Department of Manuscripts and Special Collections, Me C 4/2/5, Peter Mews to Edward Mellish, 22 July 1697; TCD, MS 750/1/77, William King to John Hough, bishop of Oxford, 8 June 1697.

8 TCD, MS 750/1/34, William King to Provost McClenaghan, 19 Nov. 1696.

9 TCD, MS 750/2/3/14–15, William King to Robert Huntington, bishop of Raphoe, 24 June 1701.

10 Suggestions that he was from Ballywalter, Co. Down, and the son of Hugh Hamill and Anne Moutray cannot be substantiated (Johnston-Liik, *History of the Irish Parliament*, iv, 323).

11 *A list of the claims*, p. 347; PRONI, T/808/6288.

12 Crawford, 'Evolution of the urban network', pp 386–7.

13 C.V. Trench, *The Wrays of Donegal, Londonderry and Antrim* (Oxford, 1945), p. 97.

14 PRONI, T/808/15293.

15 PRONI, D/1939/18/10/2.

16 PRONI, D/1854/2/19, fo. 157.

17 J. Hempton, *The siege and history of Londonderry* (Londonderry, 1861), p. 61D; Young, *Fighters of Derry*, pp 133–4; Johnston-Liik, *History of the Irish parliament*, iv, 323.

18 K.J. McKenny, 'The landed interests, political ideology and military campaigns of the north west Ulster settlers and their Lagan army in Ireland, 1641–85', PhD, State University of New York at Stony Brook (1994), p. 283.

19 NAI, Lodge MSS, vii, pp 359, 407.

20 'Abstracts of land grants under the Acts of Settlement and Explanation, 1666–84', *Reports of the Commissioners … Public Records of Ireland*, p. 110.

21 *A list of the claims*, p. 348.

22 PRONI, D/1201/75/30.

23 RDD, 4.460.1160.

24 Hamilton, *House of Hamilton*, p. 718.

25 Simington (ed.), *Civil Survey III*, pp 379, 390.

26 PRONI, D/623/B/13/8

27 Hamilton, *House of Hamilton*, p. 1027.

28 HMC *14th Report, Ormonde MSS*, p. 438.

29 Ibid., p. 22.

30 PRONI, T.307A

31 PRONI, T/934/1; T.581/1.

32 PRONI, D/1939/18/10/3.

33 A. Clarke, *Prelude to Restoration* (Cambridge, 1999), pp 180–81.

34 PRONI, T/581/1.

35 PRONI, D/623/B/13/9

36 A. Lecky, *Roots of Presbyterianism in Donegal* (Omagh, 1978), p. 200.

37 PRONI, T/808/4787.

38 PRONI, T/808/9243.

39 TCD, MS 750/2/2/85–6, King to Alexander Cairncross, n.d. [1701].

40 Moody and Simms (eds), *Bishopric of Derry and the Irish Society*, ii, p. 174; a comment beside the rental of *c.*1696

notes:'... the tenant fulfils the conditions of his lease'; *A list of the claims*, p. 350.

41 Agnew, *Belfast merchant families*, p. 36–7.

42 PRONI, T/581/3, p. 20.

43 PRONI, T/1026/6, p. 20.

44 PRONI, T/280.

45 PRONI, T/581/1.

46 PRONI, T/681, p. 387.

47 Ibid.

48 PRONI, T/581/3, p. 202.

49 PRONI, D/623/B/3/6.

50 Agnew, *Belfast merchant families*, p. 39.

51 PRONI, T/581/1.

52 Hayton, 'Exclusion, conformity, and parliamentary representation', pp 61–2; Hunter, 'Plantation of Ulster in Strabane barony', p. 32.

53 Young, *Fighters of Derry*, p. 163.

54 RDD, 11.97.4079.

55 Simington (ed.), *Civil Survey III*, p.390, 392; W.J. Roulston, *The parishes of Leckpatrick and Dunnalong: their place in history* (Letterkenny, 2000), p. 45.

56 NAI, Lodge MSS, viii, p. 96.

57 PRONI, D/3608/10/1.

58 The Act for the Relief of Protestant Purchasers was passed in 1702 in response to the massive opposition to the Act of Resumption from those who had bought or acquired fee farm interests in lands from the king's grantees in the 1690s, the 5th earl of Abercorn among them. The act gave these individuals or their representatives the opportunity of buying in their purchases at 13 times the annual rent provided that they did so by 25 March 1703. They were also allowed an abatement of one third of what they had paid to the grantees. This coupled with the £21,000 which had previously been allotted for their relief via the Act of Resumption meant that in effect they were credited with two thirds of their original outlay (J.G. Simms, *The Williamite confiscation in Ireland, 1690–1703* London, 1956, pp 127, 148).

59 Earl of Belmore, *Parliamentary memoirs of Fermanagh and Tyrone from 1613 to 1885* (Dublin, 1887), pp 365–6.

60 PRONI, T/581/1, p. 208.

61 PRONI, T/808/2485.

62 G.D. Burtchaell and T.U. Sadleir (eds), *Alumni Dublinenses, 1593–1860* (Dublin, 1935), pp 545, 753.

63 PRONI, T/280/1, p. 9.

64 *Fasti of the Irish Presbyterian Church, 1613–1840*, compiled by the late James McConnell and revised by his son the late Samuel G. McConnell (Belfast, [1951]) p. 117.

65 *Records of the General Synod of Ulster from 1691 to 1820* (3 vols, Belfast, 1891), i, 322, 329.

66 PRONI, D/623/B/13/9; RDD, 1.504.392.

67 RDD, 81.534.58654; 7.295.2434.

68 PRONI, LA/79/2AA/3B, p. 53.

69 RDD, 4.343.1019.

70 PRONI, D/1062/3/11.

71 PRONI D/1062/4/B; LPC/771; D/1118/3/9/1; RDD, 4.460.1160.

72 RDD, 4.460.1160; 10.161.3309; 70.369.48745; 24.326.13926.

73 PRONI, D/623/B/13/8.

74 RDD, 4.460.1160, 82.203.57549.

75 M. Cox, 'The Plantation and seventeenth-century developments', p. 78.

76 Barnard, *New anatomy of Ireland*, pp 129–30.

77 Malcomson, 'Politics of "natural right"', pp 49–52.

78 PRONI, LPC/1325.

4. THE CHURCHES AND RELIGIOUS CONTROVERSY

1 R. Gillespie, *Devoted people: belief and religion in early modern Ireland* (Manchester, 1997), p. 20.

2 PRONI, T/505/1.

3 TCD, MS 1995–2008/431a.

4 Simington (ed.), *Civil Survey III*, p. 389.

5 C.D. Milligan, *History of the siege of Londonderry* (Belfast, 1951), p. xiii.

6 TCD, MS 750/1/34, King to David McClenaghan, 1696.

7 Moody and Simms (eds), *Bishopric of Derry and the Irish Society*, i, 375.

8 Graham, *Derriana*, p. 43.

9 PRONI, D/1062/3/17.

10 J.B. Leslie, *Derry clergy and parishes* (Dundalk, 1937), pp 136, 257; PRONI, D/623/B/3/6.

11 Leslie, *Derry clergy and parishes*, pp 253–4.

12 Earl of Belmore, *A history of two Ulster manors* (Dublin and London, 1903), p. 393; PRONI, T/808/6174.

13 Leslie, *Derry clergy and parishes*, p. 133.

14 TCD, MS 1995–2008/368, William King to Dr Samuel Foley, 24 July 1694.

15 PRONI, D/1939/18/10/2; TCD, MS

1995–2008/368, William King to Dr Samuel Foley, 24 July 1694.

16 J. Dooher, "'Commit thy work to God": the history and times of the Sinclairs of Hollyhill' in *Concordia* 3 (1995), pp 25–6.

17 TCD, MS 750/2/2/76, Willam King to St George Ashe, 2 March 1700–01.

18 TCD, 1995–2008/1120, 6th earl of Abercorn to William King, 20 Oct. 1704.

19 'Church Miscellaneous Papers, 1652–1795', *58th Report of the Deputy Keeper of the Public Records of Ireland*, p. 78.

20 TCD, MS 1995–2008/707, John Campbell, earl of Breadalbane, to King, 25 July 1700.

21 Leslie, *Derry clergy and parishes*, p. 132.

22 HMC, *Hastings MSS,* iv, 110–11.

23 Ibid., p. 128.

24 R.L. Greaves, *God's other children: Protestant nonconformists and the emergence of denominational churches in Ireland, 1660–1700* (Stanford, 1997), p. 86.

25 PRONI, T/552, p. iv.

26 HMC, *Ormonde MSS*, n.s., vii, 58.

27 Ibid., vi, 486.

28 D.M. Butler, *Quaker meeting houses of Ireland* (Dublin, 2004), p. 191.

29 PRONI, MIC/637/6.

30 Young, *Fighters of Derry*, p. 123.

31 PRONI, MIC/637/6.

32 A.G. Lecky, *Roots of Presbyterianism in Donegal* (Omagh, 1978), p. 200.

33 RDD, 10.161.3309. The men were John Love, Hugh Brown, John Wilson, David Bradley, Andrew Carson and Robert Askin.

34 PRONI, T/581/3, pp 192, 202.

35 PRONI, T/1026/6, p. 20; D/623/B/3/6.

36 TCD, MS 750/3/2/249, William King to Oliver McCausland, 2 Oct. 1708.

37 PRONI, MF/10/1A.

38 TCD, MS 1995–2008/699, John Sinclair to William King, 23 June 1700; J.C. Beckett, *Protestant dissent in Ireland, 1687–1780* (London, 1948), p. 36.

39 TCD, MS 750/1/34, William King to [David] McClenaghan, 19 Nov. 1696; MS 750/1/156, same to same, 12 Jan. 1697–8.

40 TCD, MS 1995–2008/900, John Sinclair to William King, 1 April 1702.

41 PRONI, T/581/3, p. 192.

42 W. Graham (ed.), *The letters of Joseph Addison* (Oxford, 1941), pp 137–8.

43 D. O Doibhlin, 'Penal days' in H. Jefferies and C. Devlin (eds), *History of the diocese of Derry from earliest times* (Dublin, 2000), pp 170–1.

44 Doibhlin, 'Penal days', pp 178–9.

45 PRONI, T/808/15265.

46 O Doibhlin, 'Penal days', p. 186.

47 PRONI, D/1062/4/B.

48 Roulston, *The parishes of Leckpatrick and Dunnalong*, pp 37, 44–5.

49 Moody and Simms (eds), *Bishopric of Derry and the Irish Society*, i, 384.

50 Ibid., p. 378.

51 J. Buckley, 'The free schools of Ulster in 1673' in *Ulster Journal of Archaeology* 9:2 (April, 1903), p. 56.

52 Leslie, *Derry clergy and parishes*, pp 134, 136.

53 TCD, MS 1995–2008/403, William King to Dr Samuel Foley, 8 Feb. 1695.

54 PRONI, MIC/1/35, Donagheady vestry minute book; RDD, 86.475.61388.

55 Burtchaell and Sadleir (eds), *Alumni Dublinenses*, pp 363 527, 545, 753.